GRAND

TREES
OF
AMERICA

Our State and Champion Trees

Lisa Jorgenson

Roberts Rinehart Publishers

GRAND ☆
TREES
OF
AMERICA

A Rhino Book

Dedicated to
Perrin and Cynthia

COVER: The "General Sherman" tree, National Champion
Giant Sequoia (*Sequoia gigantea*), largest living thing on
earth. Sequoia National Park, California.
Photographs © Whit Bronaugh
Copyright © 1992 by Lisa Jorgensen

Published by Roberts Rinehart Publishers
P.O. Box 666, Niwot, Colorado 80544
International Standard Book Number 1-879373-15-7
Library of Congress Catalog Card Number 91-66677
Printed in the United States of America
Designed by Ann W. Douden

GRAND CONTENTS

National Champion Joshua Tree, San Bernardino National
Forest, California. Photo by Whit Bronaugh.

GRAND ☆ INTRO-DUCTION

How big is the largest tree? The United States has many trees that are the largest and oldest living things on the planet. These majestic trees began to grow long before humans could read or write to record when these trees were mere saplings. The old trees spread their branches and continued to grow while the pyramids were built, the Greeks and Romans raised the columns of their temples, and while the Indians signed the peace treaties, and pioneers camped under them. New legislatures adopted them as symbols of enduring strength.

Some are National Champions.

These beautiful trees still grow today. Standing at the roots of a National Champion tree gives you a sense of grandeur unequaled by any other living thing.

National Champion Valley Oak, Covelo, California.
Photo by Whit Bronaugh.

Trees reach back to a time about 150 million years ago, around the same time that dinosaurs roamed the earth. The oldest trees are the Giant Sequoias, members of the red pine family, and the magnolia tree, one of the first known plants to have petalled flowers. The following table shows when some of the first ancestral stock of trees appeared as a plant form on earth.

Giant Sequoia	150 million years ago	
Red Pine	110	
Magnolia	105	
Tulip Tree	105	
Sycamore	100	
Witchhazel	87	
Chestnut	85	
Palm	75	
Elm	60	Dinosaurs disappeared 65 million years ago
Cottonwood	60	
Dogwood	60	Climate changed from tropical to semi-dry
Maple	60	
Birch	55	First known grasses found in fossils in Kentucky and Tennessee
Palmetto	50	
Holly	50	
Pecan	45	
Spruce	40	
Buckeye	30	
Redbud	30	
Fir	30	
Hemlock	30	
Oak	30	
Pinyon Pine	20	
Bald Cypress	20	
Beech	20	

MAP: "Virgin Forests: How Much Have We Lost?"
Norse, Elliot A., "What Good Are Ancient Forests?,"
THE AMICUS JOURNAL, Vol. 12: No. 1, Natural Resource
Defense Council, New York, 1990. p. 45.
Redrawn by J. Keith Abernathy.

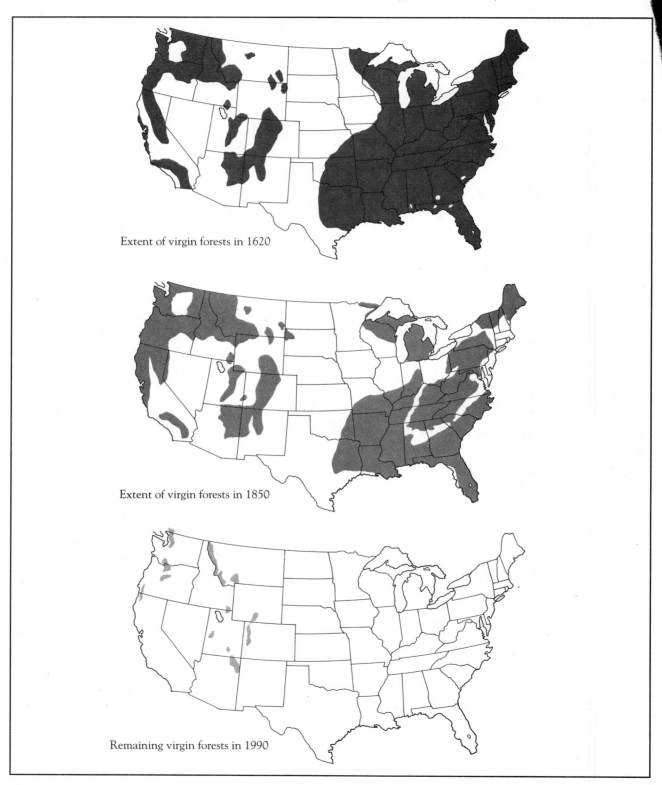

Extent of virgin forests in 1620

Extent of virgin forests in 1850

Remaining virgin forests in 1990

Information for the table on page 3 was derived from:
Muller, Jan, "Fossil Pollen Records of Extant Angiosperms,"
THE BOTANICAL REVIEW, Vol. 47: No. 1, The New
York Botanical Garden, July 2, 1981.

and with the help of the following people who are experts
on paleobotany records of trees:

Scott Wing, Natural History Museum, Washington, D.C.
202-462-1919

Charles Miller (pines) University of Montana,
406-243-5382

David Dilcher (flowers) Florida Museum of Natural History,
904-392-1721

William Carpt (grasses) Cornell University, 607-255-2131

Kevin Nixon (oaks) Cornell University, 607-255-2131

Charles Daghlian (palms) Dartmouth University,
603-646-1110

When the first colonists came from Europe three hundred years ago they found thick forests of enormous trees. In New York, they found giant maple trees. Along the banks of the Potomac River, where Washington, D.C., is now, they found magnificent magnolias.

These trees were so big that six men holding out their arms could hardly reach around the trunk. Trees of this size were a problem. They were too large to chop down or saw with hand saws. What the colonists did was to chop away a ring of bark near the base of the tree. This method of killing trees is called girding. Tree roots send water and nutrients to the leaves through the bark. By girding the bark on only two or three huge trees pioneers were able to clear an acre of land, enough space for a large vegetable garden.

Slowly these giant trees were girded, chopped, and cleared from the land. You can see the results on the map opposite this page. Primal forests once covered almost the whole country. Today the original forest still grows in only a few places.

During the 1940s, a few people became concerned that so many big trees were being cut down. Two important ideas arose.

First, many states passed laws that identified one type of tree as the state's official state symbol. Today, every state has a special tree species to represent it. Do you know what your state tree is? You can find out in the following pages.

Second, Mr. Joseph I. Sterns became concerned about the preservation of the ancient trees. Many trees were being cut to prepare the country for World War II. Mr. Stern's letters to the American Forestry Association started a campaign to find and register the largest living tree of each of the North American species found in the nation.

People who knew of large trees in their state were encouraged to write to the National Register of Big Trees, and to send the height of the tree, the measurement around the trunk at 4 ½ feet above the ground, and how wide the branches extend at the crown.

How big do you think the largest living tree is? The largest known tree is a Giant Sequoia called the General Sherman. This tree is 275 feet tall, almost the length of a football field. The circumference is 83 feet 2 inches. The estimated weight is 6,167 tons. The General Sherman tree is 3,800 years old, and is still growing.

Today, North America has 754 different species of trees, both native and naturalized, that are recorded at the National Register of Big Trees. Every year as people hear about the program, they send in measurements of other large trees. The National Register often has to revise its list when people discover even larger trees than had previously been identified. But not all the big trees have been identified. Over 200 native American trees still do not have an identified "champion."

Only five giant trees have stayed on the list since the 1940s. They are the Rocky Mountain Juniper, the Western Juniper, the White Oak, the California Sycamore, and the Giant Sequoia.

On the following pages you can read about the largest trees in the nation. Measure the largest trees you have in your yard, a nearby park, and your town. Then you will realize how really big a big tree is. Instructions for measuring a tall tree are given in the back of this book.

Maybe, you will be lucky and discover a tree that is even bigger than the trees mentioned here. If you think you have found one of our country's historic trees mail in the information using the form at the back of the book. If you find a champion, your name will be registered with the tree as the person responsible for identifying one of America's living landmarks.

STATE TREES

ALABAMA

State Tree: Southern Pine

Pinus spp.

Description:

height: to 150 feet

diameter: to 4 feet

leaves: dark green needles, 12-18 inches long

cones: conical, 6-10 inches long, wide prickly scales

bark: brown, scaled

Shape: tall with branches on upper third of trunk

Year of Designation: 1949

There are 125 species of pine known around the world, 40 of which are native to North America.

The Southern Pine is the name given as the official name of the state tree of Alabama. It is a term used by lumbermen to describe four of the eight species common in this area; the Longleaf, Loblolly, Slash, and Shortleaf Pines. The Southern Pines have a hard wood and therefore have more commercial value.

Illustrated here is the Longleaf Pine. It is a tall erect tree that grows in the interior, somewhat back from the coast, from Virginia to Florida, and inland in areas of Alabama, Louisiana, and Texas.

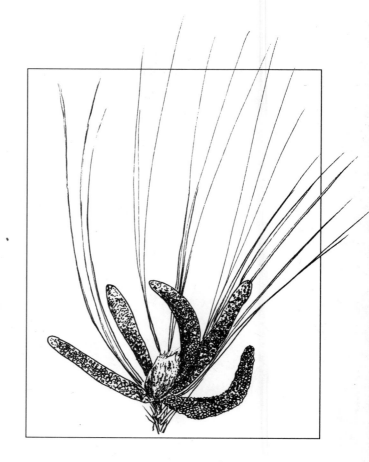

This pine has a slender trunk and a narrow crown of twisted branches that are softened by long, flexible needles that shimmer emerald green in the wind. Silver sheathes group the needles in bundles of three.

Lumber cut from the Longleaf pine, called Southern pine by builders, is strong. Its yellowish-brown color makes it a popular wood for flooring and furniture.

The wood from Southern Pines is also used to make paper. The Southern Pine region produces most of the pulp and paper in the country.

The champion Longleaf Pine is in Texas, on the Alabama-Coushatta Indian Reservation:

Circumference at 4 ½ feet (inches): 94

Height (feet): 105

Spread (feet): 42

Total Points : 210

Alabama is home to 12 national champion trees!

ALASKA

State Tree: Sitka Spruce

Picea sitchensis

Description:

height: 160-200 feet

diameter: 3-5 feet

leaves: flattened, silvery-gray needles; 1 inch

cones: oval, 2-3 inches

bark: thin, gray, smooth

shape: erect pyramid

Year of Designation: 1962

The Sitka Spruce is an evergreen tree in the pine family. Forty species are native to North America. The Sitka Spruce was named for the Alaskan capitol when Alaska was a Russian colony. It grows along the misty marine coasts of Alaska and western Canada to California, and about 50 miles inland.

The Sitka Spruce is the largest spruce in the northern hemisphere. The tree can grow as fast as 3 feet in a year. This rapid growth has made the Sitka Spruce the primary tree for reforestation in Great Britain.

Needles of this spruce are flattened and grow spirally around the twig. Spruce twigs are easily distinguished from smooth fir twigs because they retain the prickly brackets that hold the needles. Sitka Spruce have oval, light-tan cones, with wavy-edged scales.

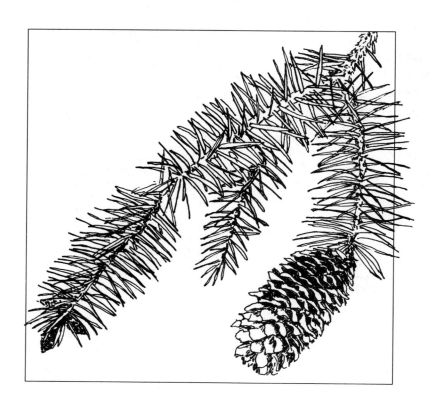

Sitka Spruce grow straight and tall in the salt spray and high winds along the Pacific coast. They are valued as ship masts and spars.

The champion Sitka Spruce is in Olympia National Forest, Washington:

Circumference at 4 ½ feet (inches): 707

Height (feet): 191

Spread (feet): 96

Total Points: 922

Alaska is home to no national champion trees.

ARIZONA

State Tree: Paloverde

Cercidium spp.

Description:

height: 20-25 feet

diameter: 1 foot

leaves: compound, 1 inch long, absent most of the year

flowers: five light-yellow petals, ½ inch wide, April-May

bark: smooth yellow-green bark

Shape: small, widely spreading

Year of Designation: 1954

The Paloverde is a small green-barked acacia that grows in the valley of the Gila River in Arizona, and in the deserts of Colorado, California and Mexico. The National Register of Big Trees records three types of of Paloverde. The state of Arizona honors all three but illustrated here is the Yellow Paloverde.

The Yellow Paloverde is a spiny tree with distinctive yellow-green smooth bark. The descending branches have almost no leaves. Thin leaves, about an inch long, unfold in March but they are gone before they mature. The vivid green, leafless branches take on the normal leaf functions of food production. In April, clusters of yellow flowers cover the branches. Seed pods ripen and fall in July.

The name Paloverde means "green hair" in Spanish noting the beautiful swags of branches swaying in the wind. American Indians living throughout the tree's range have traditionally collected and eaten the Paloverde's beanlike seeds.

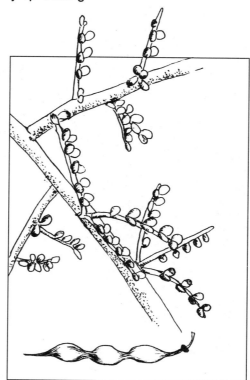

The champion Yellow Paloverde can be found in "Old Tucson," Arizona:

Circumference at 4 ½ feet (inches): 112

Height (feet): 48

Spread (feet): 66

Total Points: 177

Arizona is home to 26 national champion trees!

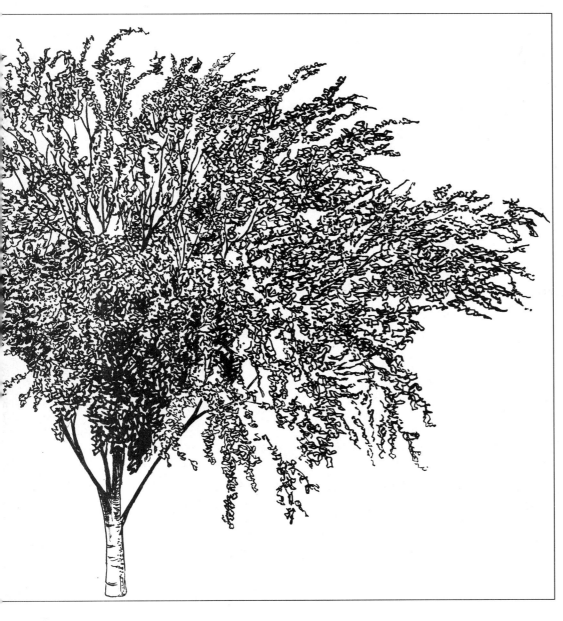

ARKANSAS

State tree: Pine
Pinus spp.

Description:

Illustrated: Longleaf Pine,
(Pinus palustris) Mill.

height: to 150 feet

diameter: to 4 feet

leaves: dark green needles, bundles of 3, 12-18 inches, cones: conical, 6-10 inches long, wide prickly scales

bark: brown, scaled

shape: tall with branches on the upper third of the trunk

Year of designation: 1939

The Longleaf Pine has a heavy, durable wood of a yellowish-brown color. Its resists decay near water making it a good wood for bridges and ship building. The sap is tapped for turpentine; tar is extracted by controlled burning.

See page 9 for details on the champion Longleaf Pine.

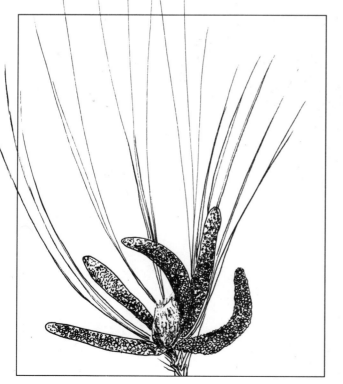

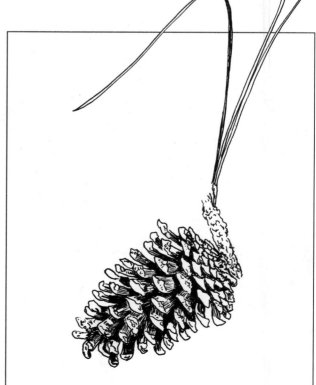

Arkansas is home to 5 national
champion trees!

CALIFORNIA

State tree: "California Redwood"; name given in state law for two species, Redwood *Sequoia sempervirens* and Giant Sequoia *Sequoiadendron giganteum*.

Description: Redwood (Illustrated)

> height: 200-325 feet
>
> diameter: 10-15 feet
>
> leaves: flat, dark green needles; ¾ inch
>
> cones: reddish-brown, short, with many scales, ½ -1 ¼ inches
>
> bark: reddish-brown, very thick, fibrous, deeply furrowed
>
> shape: world's tallest tree, buttressed at base, short open crown

Year of designation: 1937, 1953

The Redwood and Giant Sequoia are among the oldest living tree species in the world. Fossil records of these trees date back to 150 million years ago. The State of California honors both trees. The Redwoods are the tallest trees in the world. The tallest tree recorded grows to a height of 368 feet. Most trees live 400 to 500 years, but the oldest known Redwood is over 2,000 years old. The Giant Sequoia, however, is an even more ancient tree, and lives longer than any other known tree. Many Giant Sequoias growing today are more than 3,000 years old.

The Giant Sequoia once grew around the world in warm temperate zones. Since the last ice age the Giant Sequoia grows only in California, along the western slope of the Sierra Nevada Mountains. The Redwood forests are larger. They extend from California into Oregon.

The Giant Sequoia grows tall and straight, often flaring at the base to buttress its height. The bark is red and rough, graying as the tree gets older. The descending branches have blue-green, awl-like leaves that grow spirally around the twigs. Twigs bear yellow bud-like flowers on the tips. The cones are egg shaped about two to three inches long, with indented woody scales, They take two years to ripen on the tree.

The name of the Giant Sequoia comes from a Cherokee Indian named "Sequoyah," who lived in the east and transcribed the Cherokee language, but never saw one of the California trees.

The Redwood (*Sequoia sempervirens*) illustrated here has a more slender trunk and is covered with deeply furrowed reddish brown bark. Its needle-like leaves are flat like yew trees. They are dark green with thin white stripes underneath, and bear pale yellow catkins. The cones are rounder and smaller than the Giant Sequoia and seed each year.

 California is home to 75 national champion trees, including both the champion Redwood and Giant Sequoia:

Giant Sequoia:

Circumference at 4 ½ feet (inches): 998

Height (feet): 275

Spread (feet): 107

Total Points: 1300

Redwood:

Circumference at 4 ½ feet (inches): 638

Height (feet): 363

Spread (feet): 62

Total Points: 1017

COLORADO

State Tree: Blue Spruce; Colorado Blue Spruce

Picea Pungens

Description:

height: 80-100 feet

diameter: 1-3 feet

leaves: silver-blue needles, 1-1 ¼ inch long

flowers: male, yellow tinged with red; female, pale green

cones: cylindrical, 2-4 inches

bark: gray or brown, furrowed with rounded ridges

shape: bushy, conical

Year of Designation: 1939

The National Register of Big Trees reports nine species of spruce native to North America. The Blue Spruce grows at high elevations in the Rocky Mountains throughout Colorado, Utah, and Wyoming.

Spruce trees differ from pines by having solitary needles instead of needles arranged in bundles. Spruce trees can always be identified from firs by the rough prickly brackets that remain on the twigs after the needles have fallen. They also differ from fir trees by having cones that hang down instead of upright.

The Blue Spruce is a slow grower and endures hard, cold winters and hot, dry summers. It maintains a bushy shape for many years. It has short, rigid branches with stiff, pointed, blue-green needles. The heavy wax on the needles makes the tree appear silvery white and protects it from winter cold and summer heat.

The wood is resonate and prized as sounding boards for pianos and violins. It is light and elastic making it useful for boats, oars, boxes, and casts. Blue Spruce are often planted in hedges as wind breaks.

Colorado had the champion Blue Spruce until 1991. It was 191 inches around and 126 feet tall. Unfortunately, the trunk of this tree had hollowed out, making it hard to tell how old it was. The new champion grows in Utah at Ashley National Forest. It is described on page 97.

 Colorado is home to 2 national champion trees!

CONNECTICUT

State Tree: White Oak

Quercus alba L.

Description:

height: 80-100 feet

diameter: 2-3 feet

leaves: rounded lobes,
5-9 inches long

flowers: pistillated flowers grow on axils until leaves sprout. Staminate flowers are light yellow catkins that hang down from the branch tips when pinkish leaves appear.

bark: light gray, slightly furrowed

shape: wider than tall,
short trunk, gnarled branches

Year of designation:
1947

In 1687 when King James II threatened to revoke the charter of the Connecticut Colony (the territory now made up of Connecticut, Rhode Island, and Massachusetts), the document was hidden by a patriot in the hollow of a White Oak tree. This tree became known as the Charter Oak. The document it concealed became the constitution for Connecticut from 1661 to 1816. The original tree was felled by a windstorm in 1856, but every year state foresters sprout acorns that are offspring of the original tree.

White Oak trees have light green leaves rimmed with red in the spring. In the fall, the leaves turn a purplish-brown and acorns cover the ground. The cap of the White Oak acorn covers only one quarter of the acorn seed.

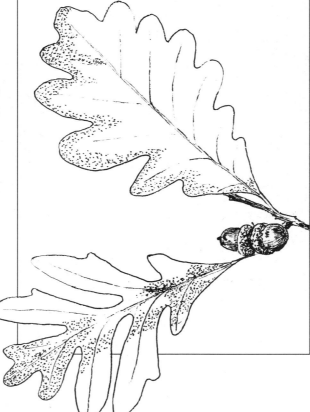

The champion White Oak can be found in Wye Mills State Park, Maryland. It is described on page 48.

 Connecticut is home to 8 national champion trees!

DELAWARE

State Tree: American Holly

Ilex opaca Ait.

Description:

height: 20-40 feet

diameter: 6-24 inches

leaves: dark green with pale green undersides; pointed, sometimes spiny-toothed evergreen; 2-4 inches

flowers: small white or greenish flowers in clusters (May-June), bright red berries (June-August)

bark: gray, thin, sometimes warty

Year of Designation: 1939

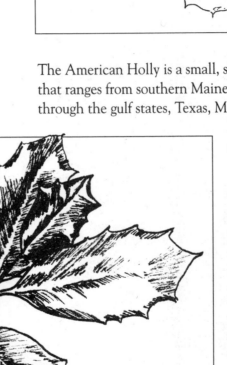

The American Holly is a small, slow-growing tree that ranges from southern Maine to Florida, and through the gulf states, Texas, Missouri, and Indiana. It requires moist, acid soils.

The tree is pyramid shaped with dense horizontal branches bearing dark green, spined leaves. The tree bears decorative red berries from late fall to winter.

American Holly trees are prized as winter decorations and for the beautiful, closely-grained white wood that resembles ivory. It is used in fine inlaid work, piano keys, and wood engraving.

The champion American Holly can be found in Chambers County, Alabama:

Circumference at 4 ½ feet (inches): 119

Height (feet): 74

Spread (feet): 48

Total Points: 205

Delaware is home to no national champion trees.

DISTRICT OF COLUMBIA

State Tree: Scarlet Oak

Quercus coccinea Muenchh.

Description:

height: 50-75 feet

diameter: 1-2 feet

leaves: deep, pointed lobes; 3-6 inches

flowers: red forked pistils, red tasselled catkins

bark: dark, finely grooved

shape: medium tall, irregular spreading crown

Year of Designation: 1960

The Scarlet Oak range extends from Maine down the eastern seaboard and into the mountains of South Carolina, and over to the Mississippi River Valley.

Oak trees can be divided into two groups: the annual and the biennial fruit-bearing species. The annuals have pale bark and leaves with rounded lobes, and the acorns mature in one year. The biennials have dark bark (the black oak group) and have leaves with pointed lobes and bristly tips. They keep their acorns on the branches for two years. The Scarlet Oak belongs to the biennial group.

The Scarlet Oak is aptly named. It has fine twigs which sprout a clear green in the spring and then turn red. In early spring, bright red leaves unfurl marking the trees' place in the forest. With the new leaves, the Scarlet Oak bears separate male and female flowers. The male catkins are clusters of long pendants with vivid yellow flowers. The female flowers are bracts of two or three green stalks near the end of the twigs.

The leaves turn glossy green with sharply pointed lobes. In the fall, the leaves are a blaze of red. The leaves of the oak cling to the branches well into the first snow.

In the fall oval acorns appear. The deep cups cover nearly half of the acorn seed. Scarlet Oaks can be distinguished by the circular lines around the tip of the acorn nut.

The wood is reddish brown and hard. It is used for flooring, furniture and many kinds of farm implements.

The champion Scarlet Oak is a resident of Hillsdale County, Michigan:

Circumference at 4 ½ feet (inches): 243

Height (feet): 117

Spread (feet): 126

Total Points: 392

The District of Columbia is home to no national champion trees.

FLORIDA

State Tree: Cabbage Palmetto

Sabal palmetto

Description:

height: 40-60 feet

diameter: 2 feet

leaves: large, fan-shaped, dark green, 4-6 feet, plus 6-7 foot leafstalk

flowers: fragrant small white, 2-2 ½ feet long borne in drooping clusters in June

bark: gray brown, smooth when tree matures

shape: slender trunk with pompom-shaped crown on upper third of tree

Year of Designation: 1953

There are 4,000 species of palm world wide. Palmettos are only very distantly related. It is known from fossil records that they developed some 25 million years later than palms. There are 15 known palmettos, but only 4 live in Florida and one is thought to be extinct.

The Cabbage Palmetto ranges along the coast from North Carolina to Florida. Palmettos are a cross between pinnate and palmate palms. Thay have large, fan-shaped leaves borne on six to seven foot stems with dark green blades shredded into long strips. The fleshy leaf bud can be eaten.

The tree is prized for its drooping clusters of fragrant white flowers. Small oval black berries ripen in the fall.

The palmetto is an extremely slow growing tree. It does not produce rings to mark its growth so it is very difficult to accurately find the age of these trees. It is estimated that large trees can be 300 to 400 years old.

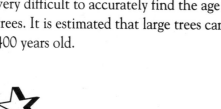

Florida is home to 104 national champion trees (more than any other state!), among them the tallest known Cabbage Palmetto, found at Highland Hammock State Park:

Circumference at 4 ½ feet (inches): 45

Height (feet): 90

Spread (feet): 14

Total Points: 139

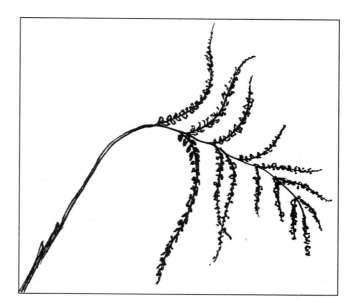

GEORGIA

State Tree: Live Oak

Quercus virginiana Mill.

Description:

height: 40-70 feet

diameter: to 8 feet

leaves: oval, evergreen, 3-5 inches

flowers: pale, inconspicuous

bark: reddish-brown, scaly, broken into fissures

shape: wider than tall, short trunk, widely spreading branches, often reaching to the ground

Year of Designation: 1937

The slow growing Live Oak is one of the majestic trees of the southern United States. When mature its branches may be twice as wide as the tree is high, and draped with Spanish moss.

The Live Oak is one of the few evergreen oaks, and cannot survive above the frost line. It has distinctive leathery elliptical leaves with smooth edges and a round base. The underside of the leaf has light gray hairs.

The acorns are blackish-brown and oblong. One-third of the nut is covered with a felty cup. The acorns ripen in one summer and are not bitter to taste.

Wood from Live Oaks is exceptionally hard and durable. Once prized for ship building, it gradually was replaced by metal.

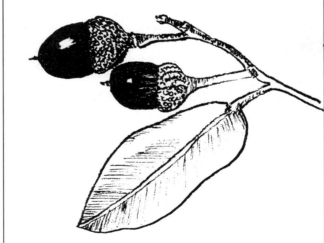

The champion Live Oak can be found near Lewisburg, Louisiana:

Circumference at 4 ½ feet (inches): 439

Height (feet): 55

Spread (feet): 132

Total Points: 527

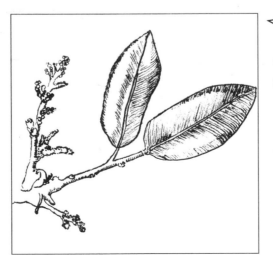

 Georgia is home to 17 national champion trees!

HAWAII

Year of Designation: 1959

State Tree: Kukui: Candlenut

Aleurites moluccana (L.) Willd.

Description:

height: 60-80 feet

diameter: 3 feet

leaves: silvery green with stout leaf stalks (often longer than leaf), leaf long, pointed, some with lobes, 4-6 inches

flowers: white clusters 3-6 inches long

bark: gray-brown, smooth with tiny fissures

shape: medium-size, full-rounded crown

The Candlenut tree grows on all the Hawaiian islands and was valued by ancient Hawaiians for light, fuel, medicine, dyes, and ornament. When President Franklin D. Roosevelt visited the Territory in 1934, a Candlenut tree was planted in commemoration on the grounds of the Iolani Palace. That tree later became the symbol of Hawaii.

The Candlenut grows to a height of 80 feet. It is easily recognized by its silvery-green leaves. White flower clusters grow six inches long. The tree produces round nuts about one to two inches around in rough shells with black marble patterns. The seeds are edible and are valued for their oil used in commercial varnishes and natural candles.

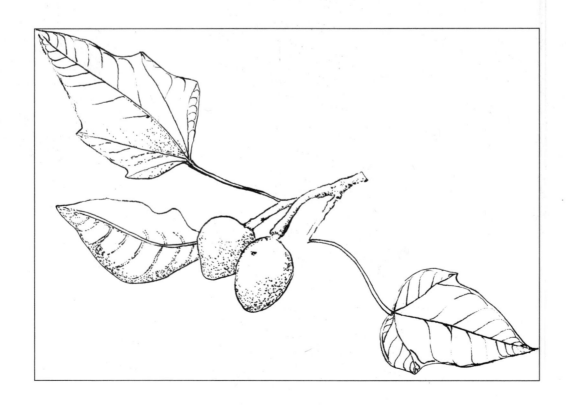

The Candlenut tree is the only state tree not native to North America. It is native to Malaya.

Hawaii is home to 5 national champion trees!

IDAHO

State Tree: Western White Pine

Pinus monticola Dougl.

Description:

> height: 100-175 feet
>
> diameter: 3 feet
>
> leaves: evergreen, blue-green needles; 2-4 inches
>
> cones: yellow-brown, cylindrical, 8 inches long
>
> bark: gray, thin, furrowed with scaly plates
>
> shape: straight trunk, narrow conical crown

Year of Designation: 1935

The Western White Pine is one of 40 species of pine native to North America. It extends from British Columbia to Idaho, through Washington, and the mountains of Oregon and California.

The Western White Pine is much taller than the Eastern Pine. Its needles stay on the tree for as long as four years, giving the crown more foliage. The tree is pyramid-shaped with groups of whorled branches.

In the spring the Western White Pine bears red catkins. Its evergreen needles are grouped in bundles of five. The tree bears long unarmed cones.

The wood from the Western White Pine is soft. It is used for construction and furniture.

The champion Western White Pine is located in El Dorado National Forest, California:

Circumference at 4 ½ feet (inches): 394

Height (feet): 151

Spread (feet): 52

Total Points: 558

Idaho is home to 17 national champion trees!

ILLINOIS

State Tree: White Oak

Quercus alba L.

Description:

height: 80-100 feet

diameter: 2-3 feet

leaves: rounded lobes,
5-9 inches long

flowers: pistillated flowers grow on axils before leaves sprout. Staminate flowers are light yellow catkins that hang down from the branch tips when pinkish leaves appear.

bark: light gray, slightly furrowed

shape: wider than tall, short trunk, gnarled branches

Year of Designation: 1973

In North America there are about 80 native species of oak, 57 of which grow to tree size.

During the spring, twigs of the White Oak have reddish-brown buds and are hung with red-rimmed, velvety leaves that are covered with silky hair. In summer, the evenly-lobed leaves turn green with lighter undersides.

In Autumn, the leaves turn a dull purple. Cup-shaped acorns cover the ground. The foliage clings to the branches well into the fall.

The branch structure and roots enable White Oaks to live 200 years or longer.

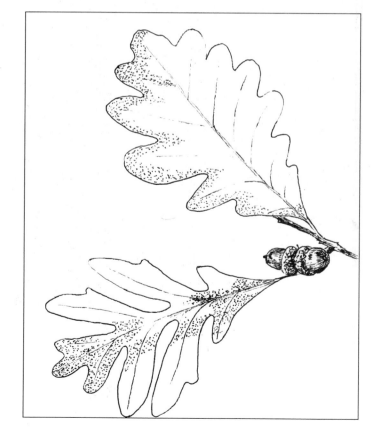

The champion White Oak can be found in Maryland. It is described on page 48.

Illinois is home to 8 national champion trees!

INDIANA

State Tree: Yellow-poplar, Tulip Poplar

Liriodendron tulipfera L.

Description:

height: 50-100 feet

diameter: 2-6 feet

leaves: four-pointed, notched, 5-6 inches

flowers: greenish with orange base, tulip shaped, 1 ½ - 2 inches, May-June

bark: light gray with grooves

shape: long upright trunk, upward reaching branches

Year of designation: 1931

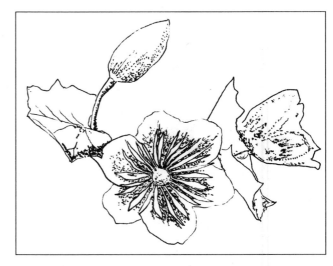

The Tulip Poplar species comes from ancestral stock 105 million years old. It is one of the first plants to develop flowers with petals to attract insects for pollenation. Its unique leaf system allowed it to survive tropical conditions, and then the ice age and semi-dry periods of history.

In the spring new leaves cup together to protect the new shoots until another leaf expands, finally uncovering a greenish yellow flower at the tip of the branch. From a waxy orange center, gold stamen protrude. Pale green leaves also appear in spring and darken later in the summer. The leaves are notched in the shape of a saddle and flutter on long slender stalks. In the fall, the leaves turn a clear yellow.

Light brown, narrow cones remain erect on the branches into the winter after they have dropped their seeds. The winter twigs are armed with oblong casings over the leaf buds.

These stately trees, 200 feet tall and ten feet in diameter, once covered the eastern seaboard and the lower Ohio River Valley. Early settlers thought Tulip Poplars were a sign of fertile land. If they cut two or three of these giant trees they could clear a nice homestead garden and the wood was light to carry away.

The wood has a soft yellow pulp. It is easily worked for local building, furniture, and harvested for high quality book paper and postcards.

The champion Yellow-Poplar can be found in Bedford, Virginia:

Circumference at 4 ½ feet (inches): 374

Height (feet): 146

Spread (feet): 73

Total Points : 551

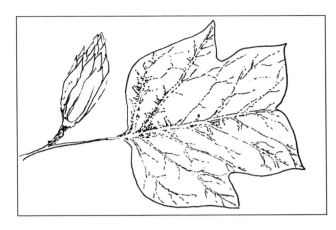

Indiana is home to 2 national champion trees!

IOWA

State Tree: Oak

Quercus spp.

Description:

height: 50-75 feet

diameter: 1-2 feet

leaves: deep, pointed lobes; 3-6 inches

flowers: red forked pistils, red tasselled catkins

bark: dark, finely grooved

shape: medium tall, irregular spreading crown

Year of Designation: 1961

Nearly 300 distinct species of oak trees are recognized, 80 of which are native to North America. Oak trees are unique because they are the only trees whose forests span the great continental divide. The state of Iowa honors all oak trees. Illustrated here is the Scarlet Oak.

The ancestral stock for oak trees is 30 million years old. This is a relatively young tree in geological history.

Oak trees are easily distinguished by their acorn cups that cling to the tree. The name comes from the Danish words, "ek korn," or oak seed used to feed pigs.

The strength and tenacity of the oak's branch structure and roots make it possible for this tree to live up to 300 years.

Because of the many species of oak in North America, there are over 70 different champions in the United States.

 Iowa is home to 2 national champion trees!

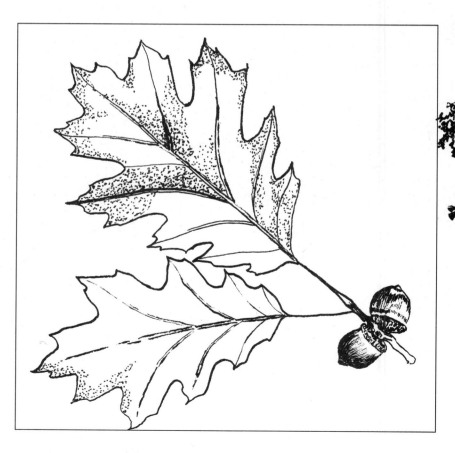

39

KANSAS

State tree: Cottonwood

Populus spp.

Description:

(Illustrated: Eastern Cottonwood)

height: 50-90 feet

diameter: 1-2 feet

leaves: lustrous light green, heart shaped, equally broad as long, 3-7 inches

flowers: male red catkins, seed pods thin walled, $\frac{2}{5}$ inches long

bark: ash gray, heavily furrowed into irregular plates

shape: wide spreading, open crown

Year of designation: 1937

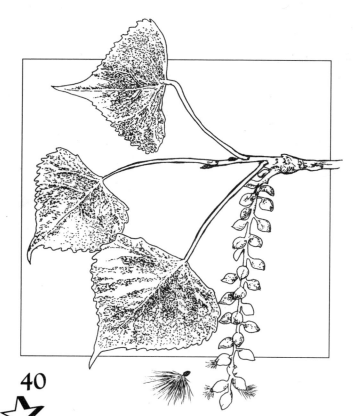

Kansas designated Cottonwood trees in general as its state tree. Illustrated here is the Eastern Cottonwood. The National Register of Big Trees records eight species of cottonwood native to North America. The Eastern Cottonwood grows along the Mississippi Valley, along the Ohio River and into Pennsylvania along Lakes Michigan and Erie to the Saint Lawrence.

Settlers and pioneers traveling west valued cottonwoods for their shade and wood for fires and building materials. Found along river banks and marshes it was a natural marker for sources of water.

In the spring red, caterpillar-like stamens flower into catkins. Fertile cottonwoods can be a nuisance when the cotton fills the air and collects on window screens.

The Eastern Cottonwood leaves are larger and more symmetrical than the Plains Cottonwood, and are distinguished by a light yellow midrib and thick coarse veins. New leaves are bright green. The foliage stays glossy and shimmers in the wind until the leaves turn golden and fall.

The wood is soft and brittle. The heartwood is dark brown and thick sap wood, pulp-like and white. Branches break easily in the wind.

A champion Eastern Cottonwood can be found in
Cassia County, Idaho:

Circumference at 4 ½ feet (inches): 433

Height (feet): 85

Spread (feet): 121

Total Points : 548

 **Kansas is home to 2 national
champion trees!**

KENTUCKY

State Tree: Kentucky Coffeetree

Gymnocladus dioicas (L.) K. Koch

Description:

height: 40-90 feet

diameter: 1-2 feet

leaves: very large, 17-36 inches

flowers: white clusters, May-June

bark: dark, scaly

shape: tall

Year of Designation: 1976

The Kentucky Coffeetree bears leathery seed pods, 5 to 10 inches long. During Colonial times and the Civil War, the ripe seeds were ground as a substitute for coffee.

Kentucky is home to 8 national champion trees, among them a Kentucky Coffeetree:

Circumference at 4 ½ feet (inches): 212

Height (feet): 78

Spread (feet): 84

Total Points: 311

The Kentucky Coffeetree is a member of the pea family. Only one of the three species is native to North America.

The tree grows from New York through Tennessee and along the bottom lands of Nebraska and Oklahoma. It tolerates drought and pollution. As it grows, the tree spreads its bushy unsymmetrical branches with their large leaves. In the spring, small white flowers appear. In the fall the tree turns a beautiful gold.

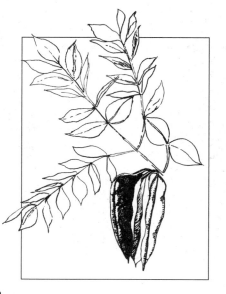

43

LOUISIANA

State Tree: Bald Cypress

Taxodium distichum (L.) Richard

Description:

    height: 80-120 feet

    diameter: 3-4 feet

    leaves: flattened, nonevergreen needles; 1 inch long

    cones: ball-shaped, 1 inch diameter

    bark: brown, smooth, fibrous

    shape: tall with distinctive swollen trunk at base

Year of Designation: 1963

Bald Cypress leaves are yellow-green, flat needles that turn brown and fall with their brackets in the autumn. The tree has round, wrinkled cones about one inch in diameter.

Bald Cypress wood is light brown and durable. In the past it was often used for doors and many of the railroad ties that built the southern railroads.

Only two species of cypress trees are native to North America. Cypress are primitive trees that grow in shallow water, breathing through protruding roots.

The trunk of the Bald Cypress has a distinct shape. It is swollen at the base with heavy fluting and narrowing as the tree goes up. The wide-spreading roots often have woody "knees" that protrude above the water.

**Louisiana is home to 6 national champion
trees, one of which is the Bald Cypress:**

Circumference at 4 ½ feet (inches): 644

Height (feet): 83

Spread (feet): 85

Total Points: 748

MAINE

State Tree: Eastern White Pine

Pinus strobus L.

Description:

height: 75-100 feet

diameter: 2-3 feet

leaves: evergreen needles, 2-4 inches

cones: curved, 4-8 inches

bark: dark, deeply furrowed

shape: tall, spreading horizontal branches at crown

Year of Designation: 1945

The White Pine, the "Mast Pine" as it is called in Maine, is described by the state legislature as "the most attractive and adaptable of the 600 species of pine." It grows everywhere in the state. In the 1600s the White Pine formed an extended primeval forest that has now disappeared. By 1820, the White Pine was the staple supply for masts to the ship building industry of England.

The White Pine is the largest conifer in the northeast, growing as tall as 100 feet. Its broad, spreading horizonal branches form a pyramidal crown. The needles grow in bundles of five.

The state flower, the red tassel of the White Pine, appears in the spring. Every two years, the tree drops its long, curved cones in the fall.

The champion White Pine is located in Michigan. It is described on page 52.

 Maine is home to 4 national champion trees!

47

MARYLAND

State Tree: White Oak

Quercus alba L.

Description:

height: 80-100 feet

diameter: 2-3 feet

leaves: rounded lobes,
5-9 inches long

flowers: pistillated flowers grow
on axils before leaves sprout.
Staminate flowers are light
yellow catkins that hang down
from the branch tips when
pinkish leaves appear.

bark: light gray, slightly furrowed

shape: wider than tall, short
trunk, gnarled branches

Year of designation: 1941

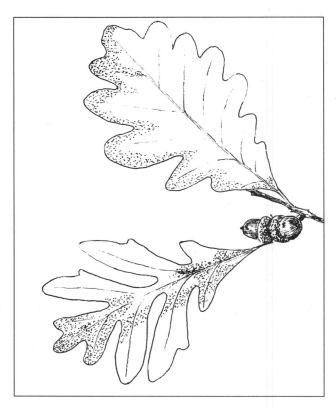

In the spring, the White Oak is hung with red-rimmed velvety leaves, covered with a silky hair. Green leaves and yellow tassels of the male flowers take their place during the summer.

In Autumn, the leaves turn violet and dull purple. The foliage clings to the branches well into the winter. Members of the Russian Orthodox Church use branches of the White Oak in their Christmas celebration. Burning branches, still covered with leaves, are swung into the sky as a reminder of the stars the wise men followed.

Maryland is home to 7 national champion trees, one of which is the champion White Oak:

Circumference at 4 ½ feet (inches): 374

height (feet): 79

spread (feet): 102

Total Points: 479

49

MASSACHUSETTS

State Tree: American Elm

Ulmus Americana

Description:

> height: 80-100 feet
>
> diameter: 2-5 feet
>
> leaves: double-toothed edges, 4-6 inches
>
> flowers: borne in drooping, short-stalked clusters of 3-4 red flowers, March-May
>
> bark: grayish, ridged in diamond shapes
>
> shape: vase shaped, trunk divides near ground, wide spreading limbs

Year of Designation: 1941

The American Elm is revered as the state tree of Massachusetts. During the Revolutionary War, colonists hung dummies of British tax collectors from a large elm tree. The tree became known as the Liberty Elm.

American Elms are gracefully spreading, vase-shaped shade trees. In March, brown buds swell along the branches and the tree appears to flush purple until the flowers scatter the seeds. Flat, greenish, paper thin seeds called "samaras" mature as the leaves unfold. The leaves are bright green during the summer, turning golden yellow in the fall.

The wood of the American Elm is characterized by interlacing fibers, making it very durable. It was once prized for boat timbers, flooring, and the hubs on one-horse open sleighs.

Since 1909, when a small European beetle arrived carrying a fungus that causes the deadly Dutch Elm disease, more than half of the elms in North America have disappeared. The fungus destroys the

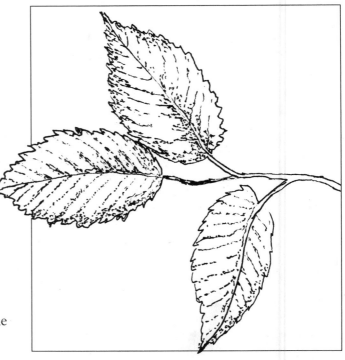

tree by cutting off the flow of liquids traveling in the bark to the limbs.

No cure for the fungus exists. However, a special disease-resistant type of elm, the American Liberty Elm, has been found. It is available through many local Boy Scout troops or by calling the Elm Research Institute at 1-800-367-3567.

The champion American Elm can be found in Louisville, Kansas:

Circumference at 4 ½ feet (inches): 312

Height (feet): 100

Spread (feet): 91

Total Points: 435

Massachusetts is home to no national champion trees.

MICHIGAN

State Tree: Eastern White Pine

Pinus strobus L.

Description:

> height: 75-100 feet
>
> diameter: 2-3 feet
>
> leaves: evergreen needles, 2-4 inches
>
> cones: curved, 4-8 inches
>
> bark: dark, deeply furrowed
>
> shape: tall, spreading horizontal branches at crown

Year of Designation: 1955

In Michigan the White Pine is valued as a smooth, light wood ideal for building. It was used to construct railroad trusses and the large grain and ore docks of the Great Lakes.

The White Pine is the only pine east of the Rocky Mountains that bears its needles in bundles of five. Belying its size and strength, the White Pine is called the "whispering pine." Its bundles of five needles create a soft wind foil. The red flower tassel and the long curved cones established these trees along the sandy path of the last great glaciers.

 Michigan is home to 76 national champion trees, one of which is the champion Eastern White Pine. It can be found in Marquette:

Circumference at 4 ½ feet (inches): 186

Height (feet): 201

Spread (feet): 52

Total Points: 400

53

MINNESOTA

State Tree: Red Pine, or Norway Pine

Pinus Resinosa Ait.

Description:

height: 50-80 feet

diameter: 1-2 feet

leaves: dark green needles,
4-6 inches

cones: thornless, 1-2 ½ inches long

bark: yellowish-red

shape: tall, erect trunk; symetrical
crown

Year of designation: 1953

The Red Pine are among the oldest known species of the pine family. They are estimated to be about 110 million years old.

The Red Pine is a tall, straight tree prized because it has few knots in its wood. The needles are dark green and grow in pairs about 6 inches long. The needles snap easily when bent. The flowers are bright red and produce long thin cones with no spines. The sturdy trunks have a red bark.

Red Pines can grow in the poorest soil and on the most exposed sites. These old trees were used as landmarks by the first fur trading voyagers who paddled along the shores of the Great Lakes.

The wood is lighter and not as full of resin as many pines. It was used by Scandinavian settlers in the early 1900s to build their log cabins. The timber also was used for huge spars and masts on vessels, and as piles in dockyards and bridges.

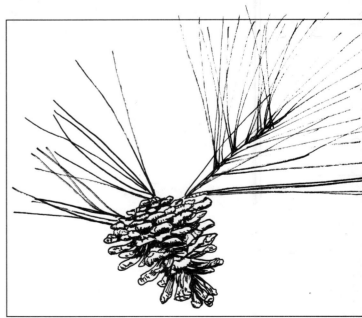

54

The champion Red Pine is a resident of Watersmeet, Michigan:

Circumference at 4 ½ feet (inches): 123

Height (feet): 154

Spread (feet): 96

Total Points: 301

Minnesota is home to only one national champion tree.

MISSISSIPPI

State Tree: Southern Magnolia

Magnolia grandiflora L.

Description:

height: 60-80 feet

diameter: 2-3 feet

leaves: oval, smooth edges,
6-8 inches

flowers: white, fragrant,
6-8 inches across, May-June

bark: gray, smoothish

shape: rounded crown

Year of Designation: 1938

The magnolia tree was named by the Swedish botanist Linnaeus for Pierre Magnola at Montpillier. Twenty-five of the 80 species of magnolia are native to North America and grow along the southeastern coastal plain from Virginia to Florida and as far west as Texas. All American species flower with the leaves or after they have come on the tree.

The Southern Magnolia is the largest and most stately. It grows to 80 feet with large, glossy evergreen leaves. The leaves are thick and have a fuzzy, cinnamon-colored underside.

The branches yield large hairy buds that open into magnificent creamy white flowers, the largest flower of any tree in cultivation. The flowers have a rich memorable smell similar to lemons.

A cucumber-shaped pistole grows in the center, and will ripen into a light brown, fuzzy cone-like structure that sticks straight up from the branch.

When the seeds ripen, shiny red seeds dangle on threads. The winter buds project up from the branches in a thick oval sheath that falls away in the spring.

Magnolia trees are among the most ancient of flowering plants. Some of the first petalled flowers to appear on earth were on magnolia trees. They have retained the same form for 105 million years.

The wood of a magnolia is tightly grained making it durable and resistant to wrapping. It is ideal for making the wood slats used in Venetian blinds.

Mississippi is home to 10 national champion trees, one of which is the champion Southern Magnolia, located in Smith County:

Circumference at 4 ½ feet (inches): 243

Height (feet): 122

Spread (feet): 63

Total Points: 381

MISSOURI

State Tree: Flowering Dogwood

Cornus Florida L.

Description:

height: 10-40 feet

diameter: 12-18 inches

leaves: egg-shaped, hairless, 2-5 inches

flowers: pink or white, 2-4 inches, March-June

bark: dark, checkered, alligator-like hide

shape: straight trunk, spreading bushy crown

Year of Designation: 1955

Dogwoods bear white or pink flowers in the spring. The four petals are arranged symmetrically and have brownish indentions. They are held at right angles to the light, and open all at one time, before the tree leaves out, forming a beautiful umbrella of flowers.

The wood of the tree is dense and closely-grained. It was prized by pioneers for its durability. Some

Flowering Dogwoods grow throughout the eastern United States from southern Maine and Michigan, into eastern Texas, and down as far as central Mexico. The trees grow best in full or partial shade.

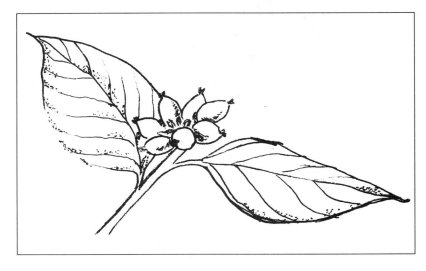

attribute the name to the wooden closures used on boats to "batten, or dog, down the hatches." In pioneer days, the wood was used for hog yokes, hay rakes, hubs and sled runners, and shuttles. Today it is prized for golf clubs and the handles of fine tools.

In the fall, the leaves of the tree turn dark red and have shiny red berries in clusters of four or five. Pioneer women used these berries to make soap.

The champion Flowering Dogwood can be found in Glenwood Park, Norfolk, Virginia:

Circumference at 4 ½ feet (inches): 110

Height (feet): 33

Spread (feet): 42

Total Points: 154

Missouri is home to 5 national champion trees!

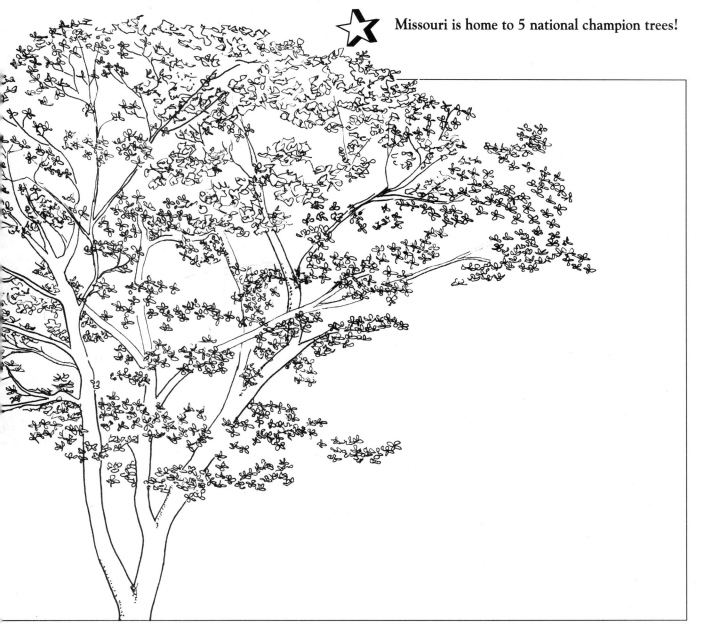

MONTANA

State Tree: Ponderosa Pine

Pinus Ponderosa Dougl ex Laws.

Description:

height: 60-130 feet

diameter: 2-4 feet

leaves: evergreen, yellow-green needles, 2-3 inches

cones: egg-shaped, reddish brown, 2-6 inches

bark: reddish orange with broad plates

shape: tall; broad, open conical crown

Year of Designation: 1949

The Ponderosa Pine forms the most extensive pine forest in the world. It grows in the mountains from British Columbia, across the continental divide, and into the highlands of Texas and Mexico.

The Ponderosa Pine grows along mountain canyons. It has short, thick, forked branches covered with yellow-green needles.

In the spring, the tree bears clusters of pink or brown flowers. The cones hide as crimson nubs at the ends of the branches until they grow, armed with prickles.

Wood from the Ponderosa Pine is light red and is a major source of construction lumber.

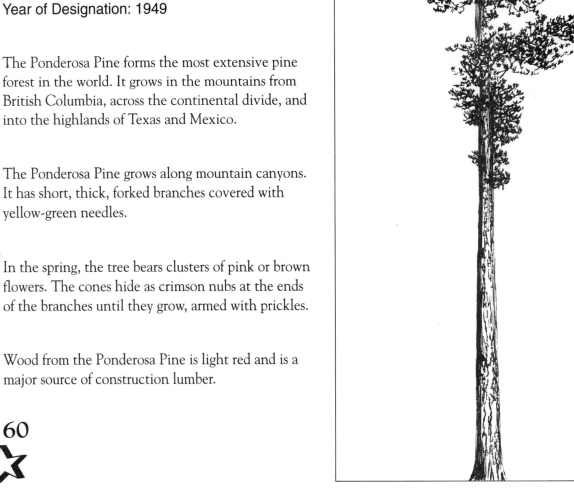

The champion Ponderosa Pine can be found in Plumas, California:

Circumference at 4 ½ feet (inches): 287

Height (feet): 223

Spread (feet): 68

Total Points: 527

Montana is home to only one national champion tree, the Western Larch.

NEBRASKA

State Tree: Cottonwood

Populus spp.

Description: (Illustrated: Plains Cottonwood)

    height: 40-75 feet

    diameter: 1-2 feet

    leaves: pale green, coarsely-toothed, heart-shaped, more broad than long, 3-3 ½ inches

    flowers: male red catkins, 2- 2 ½ inches long female catkins, 4-8 inches long-seed pods thin walled, ²/₅ inches long

    bark: ash gray, regularly divided into rounded ridges

    shape: wide-spreading, open crown

Year of Designation: 1972

Nebraska honored cottonwood trees in general as its state tree. Illustrated here is the Plains Cottonwood. Plains Cottonwoods grow naturally from Alberta to New Mexico, along the foothills of the Rocky Mountains to the eastern part of Nebraska. The Plains Cotonwood is smaller than the Eastern Cottonwood.

Lone Tree, Nebraska, was named for a great cottonwood tree that was the landmark of the Ox Bow Trail. Wagon train directions were, "Travel three days until you come to the tree."

Plains Cottonwood trees were valuable to pioneers who settled the Western Plains. They marked where water could be found, tracing out the borders of river banks and marshes. In addition, they survive cold winters and dry summers making it a valued source of shade and wood to settlers and travelers. Even today, only two percent of Nebraska is covered with trees, most of them cottonwoods.

New leaves of the Plains Cottonwood are a shiny, bright green. The foliage stays glossy and shimmers in the wind until the leaves turn golden and fall. In the spring, red caterpillar-like catkins hang down among the new leaves. Fertile Cottonwood trees fill the air with floating tasselled seeds, what the author Willa Cather called our "summer snow."

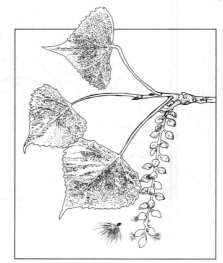

The wood is dark yellowish brown covering a thick white sapwood that is soft and pulplike. Boats could be made by burning out the center of the tree and fashioning pirogues for travelling western rivers. The Indians used the outer bark as forage for their horses in the winter. General Custer in his Arkansas campaign of 1868-1869 described how he would hunt the Indian tribes down by looking for the thick groves of cottonwood trees.

The champion Plains Cottonwood is located near the St. Vrain River in Hygiene, Colorado:

Circumference at 4 ½ feet (inches): 432

Height (feet): 105

Spread (feet): 93

Total Points: 560

Nebraska is home to one national champion tree— an Eastern Cottonwood!

NEVADA

State Tree: Singleleaf Pinyon

Pinus monophylla Torr. & Frem.

Description:

> height: 16-30 feet
>
> diameter: 1-2 feet
>
> leaves: stiff, pointed needles; 1-2 ½ inches
>
> cones: long, egg-shaped, 2-3 inches
>
> bark: brownish gray, smooth when young, furrowed when mature
>
> shape: bushy, spreading, rounded crown

Year of Designation: 1972

The Singleleaf Pinyon is the most common tree of the mountains of the Great Basin. Its forests extend from the western slopes of the Wasatch Mountains of Utah to the Sierra Nevada in California.

The tree is a broad, compact pyramid that resembles an old apple tree in shape. The short, stiff dark green needles grow singly.

The oblong cones bear one large seed under each scale. The nuts take two years to ripen. John Muir called this tree, "the bountiful orchards of the red man . . . a family can gather fifty or sixty bushels in a single month before the snow comes, and then their bread for the winter is sure." [2]

The Singleleaf Pinyon is not a commercial forest tree. The wood does not have a straight grain. It is used primarily for posts and poles. It is valued as a fire wood, especially for western mining and ore extraction. Its BTU is very high, similar to that of oak.

 Nevada is home to 3 national champion trees, one of which is a Singleleaf Pinyon located outside of Reno:

Circumference at 4 ½ feet (inches): 139

Height (feet): 53

Spread (feet): 66

Total Points: 206

[2]Rogers, Julia Ellen, *Trees Worth Knowing*, New York, Doubleday, Page and Company, 1917. p. 232

NEW HAMPSHIRE

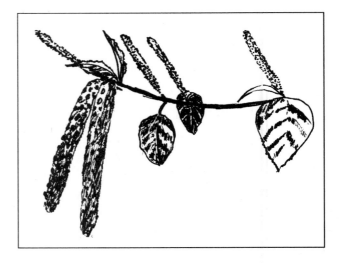

State Tree: Paper Birch

Betula papyrifera Marsh.

Description:

height: 70-80 feet

diameter: 2 feet

leaves: heart-shaped, 1-4 inches

flower: slender catkins, August-September

bark: white, peeling

shape: central trunk branching into an irregular, pyramidal, or rounded crown

Year of Designation: 1947

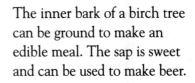

The inner bark of a birch tree can be ground to make an edible meal. The sap is sweet and can be used to make beer.

Birch wood is prized for furniture making.

Ten of the 400 species of birch live in North America. The Paper Birch is found from Alaska to Newfoundland and south across the northern tier of the United States.

The Paper Birch is known for its unusual white bark. The bark, bronze on young trees, matures to white with black fissures. In the spring, the bark can be peeled away in light, completely waterproof strips. This bark material was used to make birch bark canoes, cups, pails and writing paper. Birch bark canoes allowed fur traders to explore and map much of North America and Canada during the 1600s.

The champion Paper Birch can be found in Hartford, Maine:

Circumference at 4 ½ feet (inches): 217

Height (feet): 93

Spread (feet): 65

Total Points: 326

New Hampshire is home to only one
national champion tree, the Sweet Birch.

NEW JERSEY

State Tree: Northern Red Oak

Quercus rubra L.

Description:

height: 70-80 feet

diameter: 3-4 feet

leaves: hairless, moderately-lobed, 4-10 inches

flowers: fringed catkins droop down among half grown pink leaves, 4-5 inches

bark: dark brown, furrowed showing reddish under bark

shape: central trunk, narrow rounded crown

Year of Designation: 1950

The Red Oak forests the northern half of the eastern United States except on the coastal plains of the Southern Atlantic seaboard.

The Northern Red Oak has short, stout branches that spread to make a narrow rounded crown. In the spring, the leaves flush pink and are lined with down

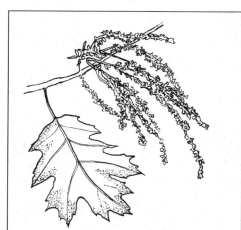

until they mature. The twigs and leaves turn a distinctive red in the fall.

The flowers are very abundant. Fringes four to five inches long dangle down in clusters from the twigs before the leaves mature. They bear large acorns set in shallow saucers. Unlike most oaks, the nut is not edible.

Wood from the Northern Red Oak is medium strong, coarse-grained, and very shock resistant. It is used for flooring, furniture, wood moldings, and mine timbers. The Northern Red Oak is the fastest growing oak tree. It grows about sixteen inches a year. It is the only oak a lumberman can plant and hope to harvest in his own lifetime.

The champion Northern Red Oak is located in Rochester, New York:

Circumference at 4 ½ feet (inches): 370

Height (feet): 66

Spread (feet): 89

Total Points: 458

New Jersey is home to only one national
champion tree, a Sand Hickory.

NEW MEXICO

State Tree: Pinyon

Pinus edulis Engelm.

Description:

height: 15-35 feet

diameter: 1-2 feet

leaves: light green needles, 1-2 inches

cones: yellow-brown, egg-shaped, sticky, 1½ - 2 inches

bark: gray to reddish-brown, rough

shape: bushy, compact, rounded, small

Year of Designation: 1949

Four species of nut pine trees are native to North America. The Pinyon pine forms extensive, open forests from the foothills of the Colorado Rockies to western Texas, Wyoming, and into Mexico. They grow in the rocky semi-arid regions of the west.

The tree has a broad compact shape that resembles an old apple tree. It has short, stiff needles that grow in bundles of two or three. Needles stay on the tree for eight or nine years.

The oblong cones bear two seeds under each scale. The nuts take one year to ripen. The nuts are rich in oil and easily keep over the winter, making them a valuable food source.

 New Mexico is home to 18 national champion trees, among them the champion Pinyon, located in the town of Cuba:

Circumference at 4½ feet (inches): 213

Height (feet): 69

Spread (feet): 52

Total Points: 295

71

NEW YORK

State Tree: Sugar Maple

Acer saccharum Marsh.

Description:

height: 40-60 feet

diameter: 1-2 feet

leaves: five pointed lobes with deep notches, 2-10 inches

flowers: greenish-yellow clusters at twig ends, April-June

bark: dark brown, rough vertical grooves

shape: short trunk, many ascending branches, symmetrical oval crown

Year of Designation: 1959

Fifteen species of maple trees are native to North America. Sugar Maples are found from Newfoundland to North Dakota and south to Georgia and Texas.

Throughout New England, Sugar Maples are among the most popular landscaping tree. They do not demand much water and can withstand disruption and confined root systems to make them ideal for street planting.

The wood is fine-grained, a pinkish-white, virtually knot free, and strong and durable. New York was a center for producing special furniture called Bird's-eye Maple from special pepper-grained Sugar Maple. It is also used for flooring, musical instruments, and

sporting goods. The wood burns at a high temperature, the same BTU as Hickory.

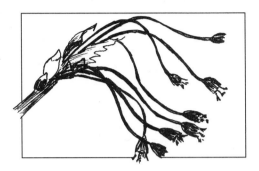

The champion Sugar Maple is in Norwich, Connecticut:

Circumference at 4½ feet (inches): 269

Height (feet): 93

Spread (feet): 80

Total Points: 382

 New York is home to 13 national champion trees!

NORTH CAROLINA

State Tree: Pine

> *Pinus spp.*

Description: Pitch Pine (Illustrated)

> *Pinus rigida*
>
> height: 20-60 feet
>
> diameter: 1-2 feet
>
> leaves: Needles twisted, yellowish green, 3-5 inches long, only pine native to northeast United States to bear its needles in bundles of three
>
> Cones: egg-shaped cones, each scale armed with sharp prickles
>
> bark: yellow-brown, rough in scaly plates

> shape: medium sized tree with ragged crown
>
> A tall tree bearing needles and cones.

Year of Designation: 1963

Around the world 125 species of pine are known. They are among the oldest and most widely distributed trees in the world. Pines grow from the Arctic Circle to Central America. In the United States, 40 species grow to tree size.

Pine trees are conifers. They have distinctive needle-shaped leaves that stay green and on the tree throughout the year. Pine trees have cones that protect the seeds until they are ripe.

Pines can be divided into two main groups: soft, or white pine, with five needles grouped together in a bundle, and hard or yellow pines, with two needles growing in a bundle.

In North Carolina, the most populous species are hard pines such as the Shortleaf Pine and the Loblolly Pine that grow in the eastern half of the state. In the far western part of the state, the Eastern White Pine grows, which is a soft-wood variety, and the Pitch Pine known for its hard resinous wood harvested for building.

 North Carolina is home to 22 national champion trees, among them two species of Pine: the Pond Pine and the Table Mountain Pine.

75

NORTH DAKOTA

State Tree: American Elm

Ulmus americana L.

Description:

height: 80-120 feet

diameter: 2-5 feet

leaves: double-toothed edges, 4-6 inches

flowers: drooping, short-stalked clusters of 3-4 red flowers, bearing wafer-thin fruits before the leaves, May

bark: grayish, ridged in diamond shapes

shape: vase-shaped, or straight trunk with wide-spreading limbs

Year of Designation: 1947

The Elm has nine species indigenous to North America. The American Elm in North Dakota is a symbol of gentle cities with green summer parks and wide tree-lined streets. Many trees were planted by the first settlers of the Great Plains.

The leaves are bright green and grow from four to six inches long and alternate along the branches. In the fall they turn golden yellow. The bark is dark gray with ridges forming roughly diamond shaped areas.

American elms as they grow in forested areas of the midwest are not gracefully spreading, vase-shaped trees but are more likely to have strong central

trunks that rise fifty feet before they branch. This makes them ideal for lumber. In 1946, more than 200,000,000 board feet of lumber was cut, most of it from Ohio and Wisconsin.

The wood is characterized by interlacing fibers, making it both very durable and flexible, hard to split, and medium weight. This made it ideal for the hubs of pioneer wagons. It was also used for agricultural implements, barrels and crates.

Historically, there have been many famous American Elms. The largest recorded elm, the Markham Elm in Avon, New York, was fifty feet in girth and about 654 years old when it fell. The national champion, now in Kansas (see page 51) is isolated from trees infected by Dutch Elm disease.

North Dakota is home to no national champion trees.

OHIO

State Tree: Ohio Buckeye

Aesculus glabra Willd.

Description:

height: to 40 feet

diameter: 2 feet

leaves: compound, 4-5 inches

flowers: yellow clusters, calyx bell-shaped long stamens, ½-1 ½ inches, early spring

bark: dark, scaly

shape: central trunk, rounded crown

Year of Designation: 1953

Buckeye trees belong to the Chestnut Tree family. Thirteen species of buckeyes are known.

Like the chestnut, the buckeye bears candelabra-like flower clusters. The Ohio Buckeye has showy yellow flowers in the spring, borne in erect 4-6 inch spikes that appear at the same time as the leaves. The compound leaves have toothed edges that turn yellow in the fall.

The name comes from the shiny red nut that is marked with a white patch reminiscent of a deer eye. The husk of the fruit is leathery with protruding bumps and splits into three equal parts dropping as many as three nuts. The nuts are poisonous.

The champion Ohio Buckeye is in Liberty, Kentucky:

Circumference at 4 ½ feet (inches): 146

Height (feet): 144

Spread (feet): 32

Total Points: 298

 Ohio is home to 9 national champion trees!

OKLAHOMA

State Tree: Eastern Redbud

Cercis canadensis L.

Description:

    height: 20-40 feet

    diameter: 10-12 inches

    leaves: heart-shaped, smooth, 2-6 inches

    flowers: pink to lavender in clusters, March-May

    bark: dark with fine grooves

    shape: branching shrub shape

Year of Designation: 1937

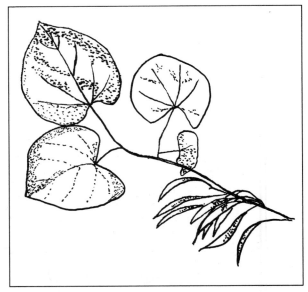

The Eastern Redbud is a small tree of the pea family. It grows from New Jersey to Florida and as far west as Ontario and Nebraska.

The National Register of Big Trees records three species of redbud native to North America. The Eastern Redbud is easily identified by its beautiful pea-like red buds forming along the length of the twigs before the leaves appear, opening into small clusters of pink to lavender flowers. The flowers are edible.

The leaves are broad and heart-shaped. They cover the tree and turn a clear yellow in the fall. Dainty tapered seed pods appear and turn purple as they ripen, and remain on the tree until spring.

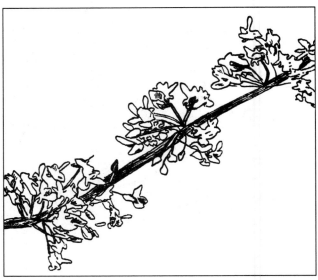

The wood of the Eastern Redbud is hard, closely grained with a darker red-brown heartwood. It is not used commercially.

The champion Eastern Redbud can be found in the city of Nashville, Tennessee:

Circumference at 4 ½ feet (inches): 120

Height (feet): 36

Spread (feet): 27

Total Points: 163

Oklahoma is home to no national champion trees.

OREGON

State Tree: Douglas Fir

*Pseudotsuga menziesii (Mirb.)
Franco*

Description:

height: 80-200 feet

diameter: 2-5 feet

leaves: short, flexible needles with rounded tip; ¾ -1 ½ inches

cones: narrow egg-shaped, 2-3 inches

bark: reddish-brown, thick, deeply furrowed

shape: very tall, narrow crown with drooping branches

Year of Designation: 1939

The Douglas Fir was named by twentyfive-year-old botanist David Douglas on his voyage along the Pacific northwest coast in 1823. The tree was first called a "false hemlock." Now it is recognized as one of a family of three firs; the other two are native to east Asia. Thick forests of Douglas Fir cover states from the Pacific Coast to the Rocky Mountains, and from British Columbia south to northern Mexico.

The Douglas Fir ranks as one of the giants in the forests of the Pacific Coast. In 1895, a tree 417 feet tall was felled in Vancouver Island, British Columbia. That tree was much taller than any recorded tree standing today. Douglas Firs are fast growing trees. The largest tree growing today is 298 feet tall and thirty seven-feet in diameter.

The tree bears short, stiff needles that spike all around the branch and pendant cones with distinct three-pointed bracts that wave beneath the scales of the cone.

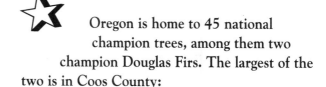

Oregon is home to 45 national champion trees, among them two champion Douglas Firs. The largest of the two is in Coos County:

Circumference at 4 ½ feet (inches): 438

Height (feet): 329

Spread (feet): 60

Total Points: 782

The Douglas Fir, called red or yellow fir in the lumber trade, is strong and used for construction and as railroad ties.

PENNSYLVANIA

State Tree: Eastern Hemlock

Tsuga canadensis (L.) Carr.

Description:

height: 60-70 feet

diameter: 2-3 feet

leaves: flat needles, ¼ inch

cones: brown, few scales, ⅝ -1 inch

bark: dark, rough

shape: loose, irregular pyramid

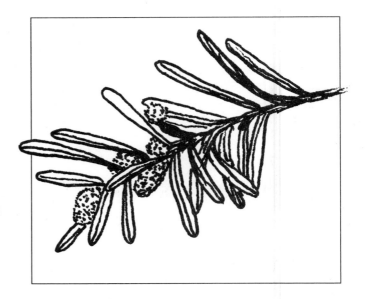

Year of Designation: 1931

Pennsylvania is home to 9 national champion trees!

The Eastern Hemlock is one of ten species of hemlock native to North America. It extends from Maine across to the Great Lakes and down the eastern mountain ranges.

The flat needles taper slightly to a round tip and give the tree a soft, lacy appearance. The branches grow upward and droop down at the tips. A small oval cone grows from the tips of the twigs.

The champion Eastern Hemlock grows in Aurora, West Virginia:

Circumference at 4 ½ feet (inches): 224

Height (feet): 123

Spread (feet): 68

Total Points: 364

85

RHODE ISLAND

State Tree: Red Maple

Acer rubrum L.

Description:

height: 20-40 feet

diameter: 1-2 feet

leaves: 3-5 lobed, hairless, 2-8 inches long

flowers: yellow, short clusters, March-May

bark: gray, smooth

shape: short trunk, full oval crown

Year of Designation: 1964

About 150 species of Maple live in the Northern Hemisphere; thirteen are native to North America.

The Red Maple bears red and yellow flowers in clusters before the leaves appear. All maples have distinctive U-shaped keys, or samara, that bear the seeds in pairs.

The Red Maple is named for its red-colored twigs, buds, and the beautiful leaves that turn scarlet in the fall.

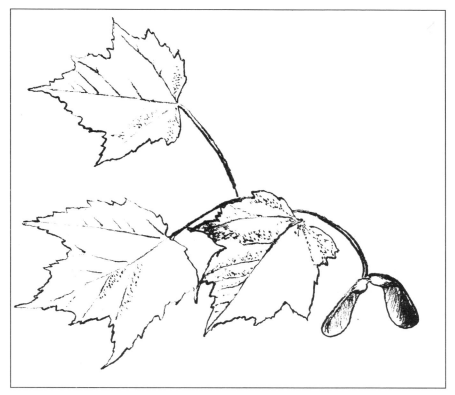

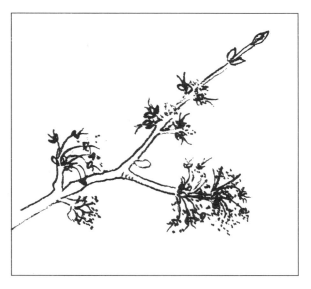

The champion Red Maple can be found in St. Clair County, Michigan:

Circumference at 4 $\frac{1}{2}$ feet (inches): 222

Height (feet): 179

Spread (feet): 120

Total Points: 431

 Rhode Island is home to only one national champion tree, the Pussy Willow.

SOUTH CAROLINA

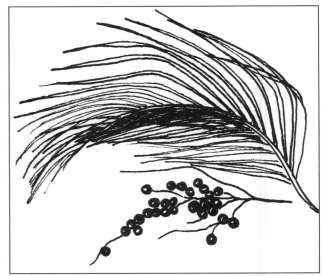

State Tree: Cabbage Palmetto

Sabal palmetto (Walt.) Lodd.

Description:

height: 40-60 feet

diameter: 2 feet

leaves: large, fan-shaped, dark green, 4-6 feet, plus 6-7 foot leafstalk

flowers: fragrant small white, 2-2 ½ feet long borne in drooping clusters, June

bark: gray brown, smooth when tree matures

shape: slender trunk with pompom shaped crown on upper third of tree

Year of Designation: 1939

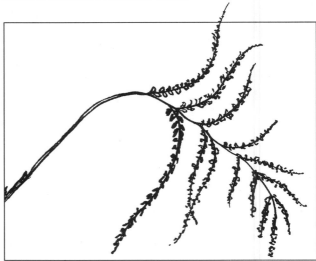

The Cabbage Palmetto grows along the Atlantic coast from North Carolina to Florida. It is one of the most common palms found in South Carolina, more often found as a bush than in its tree form.

Palmettos are only distantly connected to the palm family. Palmetto leaves are a cross between pinnate and palmate leaf. The Cabbage Palmetto has large fan-shaped leaves, borne on six to seven foot stems with dark green blades shredded into long strips.

The heart of the leaf bud is edible and commonly called "swamp cabbage". However, taking the bud will kill the tree. Even small Cabbage Palmettos can

be old trees. The Cabbage Palmetto will stay in a supressed bush form for four to twenty years growing on the forest floor until it can have open sun. The palmetto is an extremely slow grower, perhaps less than one inch per year.

The tree is prized for its drooping clusters of fragrant white flowers. Small oval black berries ripen in the fall.

Cabbage Palmetto is covered with dried leaf bases until the trunk matures and becomes a smooth gray-

brown at the base.
The wood from
Cabbage Palmettos is
used for wharf piles.

A champion Cabbage
Palmetto lives in
Florida. See page 27
for details.

**South Carolina is
home to 13 national
champion trees!**

SOUTH DAKOTA

State Tree: White Spruce, Black Hills Spruce

Picea glauca (Moench) Voss.

Description:

      height: 50-60 feet

      diameter: 1-2 feet

      leaves: blue-green needles, 3/4 inches

      cones: 1-2 inches

      bark: dark, rough

      shape: pyramid shaped, nearly horizontal branches

Year of Designation: 1939

Seven species of spruce are native to North America; three are native to the eastern United States. The White Spruce forms a broad transcontinental belt across the northern United States.

The Black Hills Spruce is now recognized as a special species. It has blue-green needles with four sides. The twigs, unlike most spruce, have smooth leaf brackets. The cones are short and cylindrical with scales, and ripen and fall off the tree early.

The wood of Black Hills Spruce is lightweight, and high in strength and stiffness. Like the Eastern White Spruce, it is harvested for paper.

The champion White Spruce is located in Koochiching County, Minnesota:

Circumference at 4 ½ feet (inches): 116

Height (feet): 128

Spread (feet): 25

Total Points: 250

 South Dakota is home to 2 national champion trees!

TENNESSEE

State Tree: Yellow Poplar, Tulip Poplar

Liriodendron tulipifera L.

Description:

> height: 50-100 feet
>
> diameter: 2-6 feet
>
> leaves: four-pointed, notched, 5-6 inches
>
> flowers: greenish with orange base, tulip shaped, 1 ½ - 2 inches, May-June
>
> bark: light gray with grooves
>
> shape: long upright trunk, upward reaching branches

Year of designation: 1947

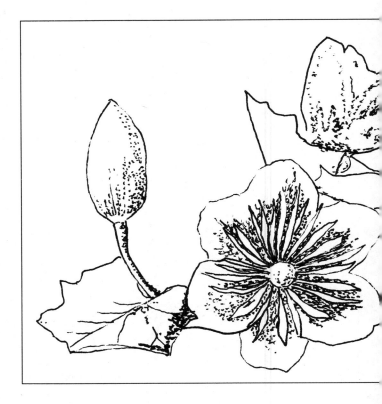

The Tulip Poplar species is unique to North America. The tree can be found from northern Florida to Massachusetts, and west to Lake Michigan and down to northern Louisiana.

In Tennessee, the soft, nearly white wood of the Tulip Poplar was called Canoewood. The wood is very light and was used by pioneers as dugout boats to ply the Ohio River. In 1775, American frontiersman Daniel Boone loaded his family and household belongings into a sixty-foot Tulip Poplar canoe and set out for the Spanish Territories.

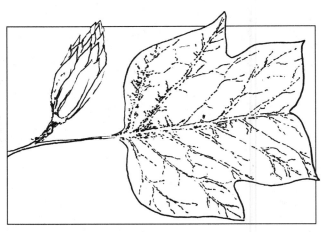

The champion Yellow Poplar, a resident of Virginia, is described on page 37.

 Tennessee is home to 15 national champion trees!

93

TEXAS

State Tree: Pecan

Carya illinoensis (Wang.) K. Koch

Description:

height: 100-120 feet

diameter: 3-4 feet

leaves: brackets 12-20 inches overall with paired leaves 4-8 inches long, smooth, dark yellowish green with lighter undersides

flowers: yellow male catkins in threes, wands 3-5 inches from branch, female flowers yellow on clustered spikes

bark: grayish brown, vertical ridges

shape: rounded crown

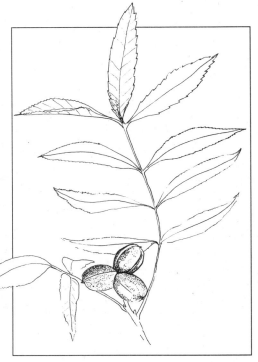

Year of Designation: 1919

Pecan trees are a subgroup of hickories. Native to the Mississippi River Valley, Pecan trees grow from Iowa down into Mexico.

Surprisingly, the Pecan tree, which grows well into the interior of the country, was discovered by Hernando De Soto only fifty years after Columbus came to America.

The Pecan tree, although one of the tallest types of Hickories, is not an important timber tree. It is planted for the commercial value of its nuts, used on ice creams and baking.

In the spring, the tree bears flowers that hang down in three branched catkins among the new leaves. When mature the leaves are paired along twelve to twenty inch brackets with nine to seventeen leaflets that turn rusty-gold in the fall. The seed pods split into four pieces, dropping smooth red-brown nuts.

Early traders and trappers first brought these nuts over the Allegheny Mountains calling them "Illinois Nuts" or "Mississippi Nuts." The trees were made popular by Thomas Jefferson and later by George Washington. The Pecan grove at Mount Vernon now represents the oldest planted trees on the plantation. When pioneer families began to move West, settlers parked their wagon trains under these giant trees where they found shade, firewood, lumber, and food.

The champion Pecan can be found in Cocke County, Texas:

Circumference at 4 ½ feet (inches): 231

Height (feet): 143

Spread (feet): 115

Total Points: 403

 Texas is home to 81 national champion trees!

UTAH

State Tree: Blue Spruce

Picea pungens Engelm.

Description:

> height: 80-100 feet
>
> diameter: 1-3 feet
>
> leaves: silver-blue needles,
> 1-1 ¼ inch long
>
> flowers: male, yellow tinged with red;
> female, pale green
>
> cones: cylindrical, 2-4 inches
>
> bark: gray or brown, furrowed with
> rounded ridges
>
> shape: bushy, conical

Year of Designation: 1939

Of the eighteen species of spruce, nine are native to North America. The Blue Spruce grows in the mountains of Utah, Colorado, western Montana and central Utah and down to New Mexico, where it endures hard, cold winters and hot, dry summers.

Spruce trees can always be identified from firs by the rough prickly brackets that remain on the twigs after the needles have fallen. They also differ from fir trees by having cones that hang down instead of upright. The spruces differ from pines by having solitary needles instead of needles arranged in bundles.

The Blue Spruce grows slowly, but at maturity can reach 100 to 150 ft.

The distinctive blue-white needles are covered by a resin that protects them during times of drought. The prickly needles bush all around the twig. A cross section of a needle is diamond-shaped.

Blue Spruce cones are three and one half inches long, light brown, and have paper-thin scales with ragged points.

Blue Spruce wood is soft, straight-grained, and valuable as lumber.

 Utah is home to 5 national champion trees, among them the champion Blue Spruce, found in Ashley National Forest:

Circumference at 4 ½ feet (inches): 186

Height (feet): 122

Spread (feet): 36

Total Points: 317

VERMONT

State Tree: Sugar Maple

Acer saccharum Marsh.

Description:

height: 40-60 feet

diameter: 1-2 feet

leaves: five-pointed lobes with deep notches, 2-10 inches

flowers: greenish yellow clusters at twig ends, April-June

bark: dark brown, rough vertical grooves

shape: short trunk, many ascending branches, symmetrical-oval crown

Year of Designation: 1949

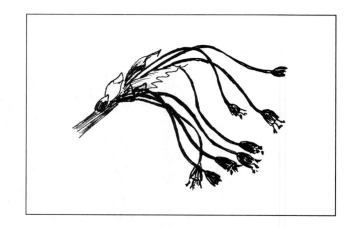

Sugar Maples are beautiful trees growing to ninty feet and producing maple syrup. Indians along the Great Lakes and St. Lawrence River originally harvested the sap. Vermont is the largest state producer of maple syrup in the country.

Sugar Maple sap is tasteless. It contains only three percent sucrose. Each year one tree produces ten to twentyfive gallons of sap. One tree can only produce about one-half a gallon of maple syrup. During the 1850s maple sugar was the chief form of sweetener for food.

The wood is used for furniture, flooring, musical instruments, and sporting goods.

The champion Sugar Maple, located in Connecticut, is described on page 73.

Vermont claims only one national champion tree, a Roundleaf Serviceberry.

99

VIRGINIA

State tree: Flowering Dogwood

Cornus florida L.

Description:

        height: 10-40 feet

        diameter: 12-18 inches

        leaves: egg-shaped, hairless, 2-5 inches

        flowers: pink or white, 2-4 inches, March-June

        bark: dark, checkered-like alligator hide

        shape: straight trunk, spreading crown

Year of designation: 1918, 1956

Flowering Dogwoods are prized trees in gardens. Their beautiful pink or white flowers bloom in April. Some people call the Flowering Dogwood a passion tree because the four petals with brown indented markings on the edge remind them of a cross. The leaves turn red with bright shiny red berries in the fall.

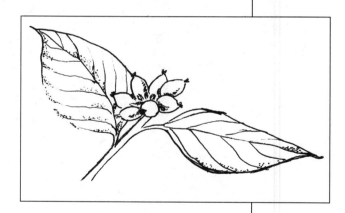

Many years ago, dogwood trees were valued as the best wood for making the shafts of arrows.

 Virginia is home to 56 national champion trees, one of which is a Flowering Dogwood! It can be found at Glenwood Park in Norfolk:

Circumference at 4 ½ feet (inches): 110

Height (feet): 33

Spread (feet): 42

Total Points: 154

WASHINGTON

State Tree: Western Hemlock

Tsuga heterophylla (Raf.) Sarg.

Description:

  height: 100-150 feet

  diameter: 3-4 feet

  leaves: flat, flexible, dark green needles, ¼-¾ inch

  cones: short, brown, ¾-1 inch

  bark: reddish-brown, deeply furrowed

  shape: tall, narrow conical crown, slightly drooping branches

Year of Designation: 1947

The Western Hemlock was chosen for Washington because of the heavy forests found in the state. This tree was later to become the backbone of the timber industry.

The Western Hemlock is the largest hemlock growing in North America. It is found from southeastern Alaska to central California, and east into Montana and Idaho. It lives in the moist lowlands and at elevations that exceed a mile.

Western Hemlocks can grow as tall as 175 feet and six feet in diameter. The crown has heavy, drooping branches that hold out feathery tips as gracefully in old age as a young sapling.

The tree's short needles are arranged in flat pairs along a short leaf stem. They are rounded at the tips, dark green and shiny, with white bands. In the spring, distinctive reddish brown, slender buds form and female flowers that look like little purple brushes form on the tip of the branch. Male flowers hang down in yellow bunches. Light brown, egg-shaped cones hang down from the tips of the branches. The cones have interesting three-pointed bracts.

Western Hemlock wood is the most durable of the Hemlock family. It is hard and yellowish brown. It is used chiefly in buildings. The bark is used for tanning.

Washington's only national champion tree is a Western Hemlock. It and two co-champions are found in Olympic National Park:

Circumference at 4 ½ feet (inches): 270

Height (feet): 241

Spread (feet): 67

Total Points: 528

WEST VIRGINIA

State Tree: Sugar Maple

Acer saccharum Marsh.

Description:

height: 40-60 feet

diameter: 1-2 feet

leaves: five-pointed lobes with deep notches, 2-10 inches

flowers: greenish yellow clusters at twig ends, April-June

bark: dark brown, rough vertical grooves

shape: short trunk, many ascending branches, symmetrical-oval crown

Year of Designation: 1949

Maple trees have 120 species, fifteen of which are native to North America.

Sugar Maples are beautiful trees growing to ninety feet and producing maple syrup. Of the thirteen states that produce maple syrup, West Virginia is not a major producer. The syrup production comes in areas where there is a predictable hard frost with warming during the early spring days to accelerate the flow of sap from the roots to form new leaves.

In West Virginia, Sugar Maples are known for their mountain beauty. It is a slow-growing tree, but can adapt well to rocky terrain with little water. In the spring in the mountains Sugar Maples take on a soft green as the new leaves and yellow flowers come out. In the fall the leaves are unsurpassed for the brilliant red-orange and yellow colors.

Leaves of the Sugar Maple have five lobes with pointed ends. The seed is U-shaped and spins down with gyroscopic motion in the fall.

The champion Sugar Maple is described on page 73.

 West Virginia is home to 4 national champion trees!

105

WISCONSIN

State Tree: Sugar Maple

Acer saccharum Marsh.

Description:

height: 40-60 feet

diameter: 1-2 feet

leaves: five-pointed lobes with deep notches, 2-10 inches

flowers: greenish yellow clusters at twig ends, April-June

bark: dark brown, rough vertical grooves

shape: short trunk, many ascending branches, symmetrical-oval crown

Year of Designation: 1949

The ancestral stock of Maple trees emerged sixty million years ago, just after the dinosaurs disappeared. The National Register of Big Trees records fifteen species of maple tree native to the United States.

Sugar Maples are beautiful trees that produce maple syrup. Indians along the Great Lakes and Saint Lawrence River originally harvested the sap. Of the thirteen states that produce maple syrup, Wisconsin is a medium-sized producer.

The champion Sugar Maple is described on page 73.

Wisconsin is home to 4 national champion trees!

107

WYOMING

State Tree: Plains Cottonwood

Populus deltoides spp. W. Bartram

Description:

height: 40-75 feet

diameter: 1-2 feet

leaves: pale green, coarsely-toothed, heart-shaped, broader than long, 3-3 ½ inches

flowers: male red catkins, 2- 2 ½ inches long-female catkins, 4-8 inches long-seed pods thin walled, $\frac{2}{5}$ inches

bark: ash gray, regularly divided into rounded ridges

shape: wide spreading, open crown

Year of Designation: 1947, 1961

The ancestral stock of cottonwoods dates back to the end of the age of dinosaurs, sixty million years ago. The Plains Cottonwood is one of eight cottonwood trees native to North America. The Plains Cottonwood today grows naturally along the streams on the great prairies from Alberta to New Mexico, along the foothills of the Rocky Mountains to the eastern part of Nebraska.

In Wyoming, whose name comes from the Delaware Indian word meaning "The Large Plains," cottonwoods are a prized tree. They can survive cold winters and dry summers, making them a valued source of shade and wood to settlers and travelers in the western plains. Groves of cottonwood trees were the landmarks of the Oregon and Santa Fe Trails because they marked where water and wood could be found. The Indians taught the early trappers and explorers to feed their horses on the soft inner bark. The cottonwood bark was also used by the Indians to bake the clay used in paints for symbolic occasions.

Plains Cottonwood is a smaller tree than the eastern species. The leaves are thick, about three inches long, and are heart-shaped on flattened stalks that let them flutter in the wind.

In the spring-red caterpillar-like female flowers hang among the new leaves in 4-8 inch catkins. Fertile Cottonwood trees fill the air with cotton fluff carrying the seeds.

The wood is soft pulp and is used for boxes, matches, and paper.

The champion Plains Cottonwood can be found in Hygiene, Colorado. It is described on page 63.

 Wyoming is home to no national champion trees.

★ SPECIES WITHOUT CHAMPIONS

Acacia

    Cinnecord, *Acacia choriophylla*

    Guajillo, *Acacia berlandieri*

    Huisachillo, *Acacia tortuosa*

    Koa, *Acacia koa*

    Long-spine, *Acacia macracantha*

    Roemer catclaw, *Acacia roemeriana*

Alder

    European, *Alnus glutinosa*

Anise

    Yellow, *Illicium parviflorum*

Apple

    Soulard Crab, *Malus x soulardii*

Apricot

    Desert, *Prunus fermontii*

Araucaria

    Cunningham, *Araucaria cunninghamii*

Ash

    Chihuahua, *Fraxinus papillosa*

    Fragrant, *Fraxinus cuspidata*

    Goodding, *Fraxinus gooddingii*

    Gregg, *Fraxinus greggii*

Bayberry

    Evergreen, *Myrica heterophylla*

    Northern, *Myrica pensylvanica*

    Odorless, *Myrica inodora*

Baycedar

    Suriana maritima

Birch

    Alaska Paper, *Betula papyrifera var. neoalaskana*

    Kenai, *Betula papyrifera var. kenaica*

Bitterbush

    Picramnia pentandra

Black-Calabash

    Amphitecna latifolia

Blackbead

    Guadeloupe, *Pithecellobium quadalupense*

Bucida

    Oxhorn, *Bucida buceras*

Buckthorn

    Birchleaf, *Rhamnus betulifolia*

Burningbush

    Western, *Euonymus occidentalis*

Bursera

    Fragrant, *Bursera fagaroides*

Caesalpinia

    Mexican, *caesalpinia mexicana*

Caper

    Limber, *Capparis flexuosa*

Cercocarpus

    Alderleaf, *Cercocartpus montanus*

    Catalina, *Cercocarpus traskiae*

    Hairy, *Cercocarpus breviflorus*

SPECIES WITHOUT CHAMPIONS

Cherry

    Alabama Black, *Prunus serotina var. alabamensis*

    Mahaleb, *Prunus mahaleb*

Chinkapin

    Ozark, *Castanea ozarkensis*

Cholla

    Jumping, *Opuntia fulgida*

Cocuplum

    Chrysobalanus icaco

Colubrina

    Coffee, *Colubrina arborescens*

    Cuba, *Colubrina cubensis*

Condalia

    Bitter, *Candalia globosa*

Coralbean

    Southwestern, *Erythrina flabelliformis*

Corkwood

    Leitneria floridana

Crossopetalum

    Florida, *Crossopetalum rhacoma*

Cypress

    Gowen, *Cupressus goveniana var. goveniana*

    Santa Cruz, *Cupressus goveniana var. abramsiana*

Cyrilla

    Littleleaf, *Cyrilla racemiflora var. parvifolia*

Dahoon

    Ilex cassine

Dammarpine

    Big, *Agathis robusta*

Dogwood

    Alternate leaf, *Cornus alternifolia*

    Smooth, *Cornus glabrata*

Douglas Fir

    Douglas Fir, *Pseudotsuga menziesii*

Downy-Myrtle

    Rhodomyrtus tomentosa

Elder

    Velvet, *Sambucus velutina*

Elephant-Tree

    Bursera microphylla

Esenbeckia

    Esenbeckia, *Esenbeckia*

Eucalyptus

    Eucalyptus

Falsebox

    Gyminda latifolia

Fiddlewood

    Citharexylum berlandieri

Fir

    California White, *Abies concolor var. lowiana*

    White, *Abies concolor*

SPECIES WITHOUT CHAMPIONS

Florida-Privet

Forestiera segregata

Forestiera

Desert-Olive, *Forestiera phillyeoides*

Texas, *Forestiera angustifolia*

Fremontia

Mexican, *Fremontodendron mexicanum*

Graytwig

Schoepfia chrysophylloides

Guava

Psidium guajava

Hackberry

Common, *Celtis occidentalis*

Hawthorn

Broadleaf, *Crataegus dilatata*

Cerro, *Crataegus erythropoda*

Fireberry, *Crataegus chrysocarpa*

Gregg, *Crataegus greggiana*

Harbison, *Crataegus harbisonii*

Hills, *Crataegus hilli*

Oneflower, *Crataegus uniflora*

Parsley, *Crataegus marshallii*

Pensacola, *Crataegus lacrimata*

Reverchon, *Crataegus reverchonii*

Texas, *Crataegus texana*

Threeflower, *Crataegus triflora*

Tracy, *Crataegus tracyi*

Willow, *Crataegus saligna*

Hercules-Club

Texas, *Zanthoxylum hirsutum*

Hibiscus

Sea, *Hibiscus tilaceus*

Shrub althea, *Hibiscus syriacus*

Hickory

Scrub, *Carya floridana*

Holacantha

Holacantha emoryi

Holly

Dune, *Ilex opaca var. arenicola*

Georgia, *Ilex longipes*

Sarvis, *Ilex amelanchier*

Hopbush

Dodoanea viscosa

Hophornbeam

Knowlton, *Ostrya knowltonii*

Huajillo

Pithcellobium pallens

Indian-Fig

Opuntia ficus-indica

Joewood

Jacquinia keyensis

Juniper

Redberry, *Juniperus erythrocarpa*

SPECIES WITHOUT CHAMPIONS

Kidneywood

    Eysenhardtia polystachya

    Texas, *Eysenhardtia texana*

Licaria

    Florida, *Licaria triandra*

Locust

    Clammy, *Robinia viscosa*

    Kelsey, *Robinia kelseyi*

Lyontree

    Lyonothamnus floribundus

Maidenbush

    Savia bahamensis

Manzanita

    Parry, *Arctostaphylos manzanita*

Maple

    Uvalde bigtooth, *Acer grandidentatum var. sinuosum*

Marlberry

    Ardisia escallonioides

Mayten

    Florida, *Maytenus phyllanthoides*

Mesquite

    Western Honey, *Prosopis glandulosa*

Mexican-Buckeye

    Ungnadia speciosa

Mountain-Ash

    Greene, *Sorbus scopulina*

Myrtle-of the-River

    Calyptranthes zuzygium

Nectandra

    Florida, *Nectandra coriacea*

Nightshade

    Mullein, *solanum erianthum*

Nolina

    Bigelow, *Nolina bigelovii*

Oak

    Ajo, *Quercus turbinella var. ajoensis*

    Britton, *Quercus brittonii*

    Bushes, *Quercus bushii*

    Caldwell, *Quercus columnaris*

    Coclut, *Quercus fontana*

    Dunn, *Quercus dunni*

    Durand, *Quercus durandii*

    Dwarf chinquapin, *Quercus prinoides*

    McDonald, *Quercus macdonaldii*

    Mohr, *Quercus mohriana*

    Sandpaper, *Quercus pungens*

    Texas, *Quercus shumardii var. texana*

    Toumey, *Quercus toumeyi*

Oleander

    Nerium oleander

Orange

    Citrus sinensis

    Sour, *Citrus aurantium*

SPECIES WITHOUT CHAMPIONS

Panama-Tree

Sterculia alata

Papaya

Carica papaya

Pawpaw

Bigflower, *Asimina obovata*

Smallflower, *Asimina parviflora*

Pine

Coulter, *Pinus coulteri*

Fallax Pinyon, *Pinus edulis var. fallax*

Virginia, *Pinus virginiana*

Pisonia

Pisonia rotundata

Plum

Flatwoods, *Prunus umbellata Ell.*

Prickly-Ash

Biscayne, *Zanthoxylum coriaceum*

Pricklypear

Brazil, *Opuntia brasiliensis*

Princewood

Exostema caribaeum

Rapanea

Florida, *Rapanea punctata*

Saguaro

Cereus giganteus

Sapium

Jumping-bean, *Sapium biloculare*

Scarletbrush

Hamelia patens

Sea-Amyris

Amyris elemifera

Serviceberry

Utah, *Amelanchier utahensis*

Shrub-Althea

Hibiscus syriacus

Silkbay

Persea borbonia var. humilis

Silverbell

Little, *Halesia parviflora*

Snowbell

Bigleaf, *Styrax grandifolius Ait.*

Sycamore, *Styrax plantanifolius*

Stopper

Boxleaf, *Eugenia foetida*

Long-Stalk, *Psidium longipes*

Red, *Eugenia rhombea*

Twinberry, *Myricanthes fragrans var. fragrans*

White, *Eugenia axillaris*

Strongback

Rough, *Bourreria radula*

Sugar-Apple

Annona squamosa

SPECIES WITHOUT CHAMPIONS

Sumac

    Kearney, *Rhus kearneyi*

    Laurel, *Rhus laurina*

    Lemonade, *Rhus integrifolia*

    Littleleaf, *Rhus microphylla*

    Mearns, *Rhus choriophylla*

Sycamore

    California, *Platanus racemosa*

Thatchpalm

    Key, *Thrinax morrissii*

Torchwood

    Balsam, *Amyris balsamifera*

Tree-Cactus

    Deering, *Cereus robinii var. deeringii*

    Key, *Cereus robinii var. robinii*

Trema

    Florida, *Trema micrantha*

    West Indies, *Trema lamarckiana*

Vauquelinia

    Fewflower, *Vauquelinia pauciflora*

Velvetseed

    Elliptic-leaf, *Guettarda elliptica*

    Roughleaf, *Guettarda scabra*

Wild-Dilly

    Manikara habamensis

Willow

    Basket, *Salix viminalis*

    Feltleaf, *Salix alaxensis*

    Florida, *Salix floridana*

    Geyer, *Salix geyerana*

    Littletree, *Salix arbusculoides*

    Mackenzie, *Salix mackenzieana*

    Northwest, *Salix sessilifolia*

    Pacific, *Salix lasiandra*

    River, *Salix fluviatilis*

    Satiny, *Salix pellita*

    Yewleaf, *Salix taxifolia*

Winterberry

    Smooth, *Ilex laevigata*

Witch-Hazel

    Ozaek, *Hamamelis vernalis Sarg.*

Yellow-Elder

    Tecoma stans

Yucca

    Aloe, *Yucca aloifolia*

    Beaked, *Yucca rostrata*

    Moundlily, *Yucca gloriosa*

    Schott, *Yucca schottii*

EIGHT EASY STEPS TO NOMINATE A NATIONAL CHAMPION BIG TREE

Every nomination submitted to the National Register of Big Trees should include the following information:

1. The correct Latin genus and species name.

2. The three required measurements described in detail.

3. The exact location of the tree, detailed enough for someone unfamiliar with the area to find it.

4. The date measured and by whom.

5. The name and address of the property owner.

6. A photograph of the tree and the date it was photographed.

7. A description of the tree's physical condition.

8. The nominator's name and mailing address.

The Three Required Big Tree Measurements

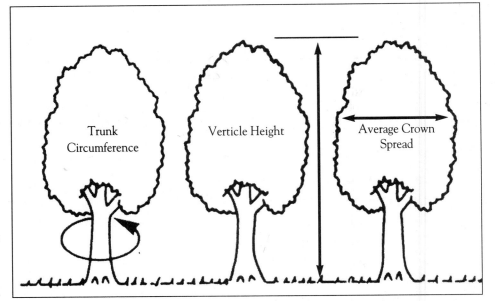

Three measurements are required when you submit the information on your Big Tree nominee. They are:

1. Trunk Circumference—The circumference of the tree is measured at 4½ feet above the center of the base of the tree. If the trunk has a growth or branch at that height or below, the circumference is measured in feet and inches at the point below 4½ feet where the circumference is least. If the ground is not level at the base of the trunk, take an average at 4½ feet. Use a string if a tape measure is not long enough.

2. Vertical Height—The total height of the tree is considered to be the distance between the base of the tree's trunk and the topmost twig of the tree.

The most reliable mesurements of tree height are made with standard measuring tools such as an Abney hand level, a hypsometer, a transit, or similar instrument.

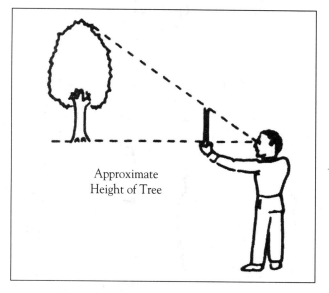

Approximate Height of Tree

However, you can also use a straight stick to get this dimension. Hold the stick at its base vertically, making certain that the length of the stick above your hand equals the distance from your hand to your eye. Staying on level ground, move away from the tree while sighting the trunk base over your hand. Stop when the top of the stick is level with the tree top.

You should be sighting over your hand to the base of the tree and, without moving anything but your eye, sighting over the top of the stick to the tree's top. Measure how far you are from the tree, and that is its height.

3. Average Crown Spread—To determine the average crown spread of the tree, trace an outline of the crown on the ground by placing stakes in the soil directly beneath the outer tips of the branches. A string with a plumb bob or other

weight attached can be used to decide where to place the stakes.

Using an imaginary line that would pass through the center of the trunk, measure the distance between the two stakes farthest apart and the two closest together on opposite sides of the tree. Add these two measurements and divide by two for the average width of the tree's crown.

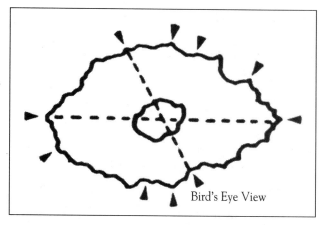

Bird's Eye View

How Trees Are Compared

To find a tree's total points, AFA uses the following calculation:

_____	Trunk Circumference (in inches)
+_____	Height (in feet)
+_____	¼ of its Average Crown Spread (in feet)
=_____	**Total Points**

A nominee will replace a registered Champion if it has more points. When two trees have scores that fall within five points of each other, they are listed as co-champions.

NATIONAL REGISTER OF BIG TREES

I want to nominate a new tree to the list of National Champion Trees living in America.

1. NAME OF TREE

a) English species name _____

b) Latin genus _____

2. MEASUREMENTS OF TREE

a) Trunk circumference 4 ½ feet above ground _____ inches

b) Vertical height from ground to tip of branches _____ feet

c) Average crown spread of limbs _____ feet long

3. LOCATION OF TREE

a) Can you locate it on a map? _____

Name of map _____

a) Nearest town _____

b) Name of nearest highway _____

c) Name of park _____

d) Name of river located near tree _____

4. DATE OF YOUR MEASUREMENTS

a) Date _____

b) Name of person who measured tree:

Name _____

Street address _____

City, state _____

Zip code _____

5. PROPERTY OWNER

Name _____

Street address _____

City, state _____

Zip code _____

6. Photograph and date of photograph

7. DESCRIPTION OF THE TREE'S PHYSICAL CONDITION

     a) Trunk and roots _____

     b) Bark _____

     c) Branches _____

     d) Leaves _____

8. NOMINATOR'S NAME AND ADDRESS

     Name _____

     Street address _____

     City, state _____

     Zip code _____

     Telephone numbe _____

Copy this form and return it to the address below. You should have a response back from the American Forestry Association within six weeks. If you have not heard from the National Register of Big Trees and you want to check on your tree nomination, call 202-667-3300.

GOOD LUCK!

NEW TREE NOMINATIONS

The National Register of Big Trees

American Forestry Association

P.O. Box 2000

Washington, D.C.

20013

582.16
JOR

Jorgenson, Lisa

Grand trees of
America

39545000659242

$8.95

DATE			